REFLECTIONS
OF A
GRIEVING SPOUSE

H. NORMAN WRIGHT

HARVEST HOUSE PUBLISHERS
EUGENE, OREGON

Cover photo © Pat Powers and Cherryl Schafer / Stockbyte / Almay

Cover by Dugan Design Group, Bloomington, Minnesota

REFLECTIONS OF A GRIEVING SPOUSE
Copyright © 2009 by H. Norman Wright
Published by Harvest House Publishers
Eugene, Oregon 97402
www.harvesthousepublishers.com

Library of Congress Cataloging-in-Publication Data
Wright, H. Norman.
Reflections of a grieving spouse / H. Norman Wright.
 p. cm.
Includes bibliographical references.
ISBN 978-0-7369-2654-6 (pbk.)
ISBN 978-0-7369-3399-5 (eBook)
 1. Bereavement—Religious aspects—Christianity. 2. Grief—Religious aspects—Christianity.
3. Widows—Religious life. 4. Widowers—Religious life. 5. Wright, H. Norman. I. Title.
BV4908.W75 2009
248.8'66092—dc22
                                                                    2008049431

Printed in the United States of America

12 13 14 15 16 17 / BP-SK / 10 9 8 7 6 5 4

In memory of
Joycelin Faith Wright and Carrie Elizabeth Oliver.

Life is full of enriching experiences, and marriage holds
the potential for the greatest of them.
My close friend Gary Oliver and I were blessed by wives
who enhanced, enriched, and changed our lives.
Joyce and Carrie taught us how to live life...
as well as how to embrace death.

CONTENTS

JOY IN MY LIFE

This is a book I never planned to write or ever even wanted to write. We're all aware death will invade our lives at some time, but it's never to our liking. The loss of a beloved partner who has been by your side for a short time or for almost half a century, as in my case, creates a Grand Canyon-sized hole in your life. The present and future are changed drastically.

I'm thankful that my wife, Joyce, was such an integral part of my existence for so long because her presence enriched my life and helped me become a different—a better—person. Let me tell you about her.

Joyce often went by "Joy," which was so fitting because she brought happiness into so many lives. Her life reflected the qualities mentioned in Colossians 3:12: compassion, kindness, humility, gentleness, and patience. As she taught the people around her much about living through her life, she also taught us through the dying process as she embarked on her next journey and entered her true home.

Beginning at a young age, Joyce loved music and art. She studied violin and sang in various choral groups. Perhaps the highlight of her singing was being in the choir for the 1985 Billy Graham Crusade held in Anaheim, California. What most never knew was that she was also a gifted artist. Joyce never really had the opportunity to develop this potential, but what paintings she completed were of great quality.

Joyce attended Westmont College in Santa Barbara, California, for the purpose of taking just the classes she was interested in. But what she really discovered there was me! She returned to Glendale, where she got a job with Lawry's Foods. She attended Hollywood Presbyterian Church and was active in the college-age group. That was when we began to date seriously, and a year later we were married in the chapel.

We had two children Joyce dearly loved: Sheryl and Matthew. Our son was severely mentally retarded and died at the age of 22 in 1990. Although the circumstances were difficult, Joyce managed with flying colors. She did everything possible to give Matthew a fulfilling life. In turn, Matthew enriched our lives and our ministry. We loved him.

Our daughter, Sheryl, was such a blessing. She and Joyce had a very close relationship and ministered to each other in times of need. And when Sheryl blessed Joyce and me with a lovely granddaughter, our delight knew no bounds. Joyce loved spending time with little Shaelyn.

Today Sheryl and Shaelyn continue to bring joy and comfort and companionship into my life. We spend as much time together as possible as we play with the dogs, pet the cat, go fishing, and talk.

Joyce's life was also characterized by her heart of love, service, grace, and care for others. On one hand she was known as being quiet and reserved when in a group, but she became very personable and caring when ministering to people one-on-one. The best word to describe who she was is *gracious*. Many have said they could confide in her because she was someone they could trust. One person commented:

> Joyce's eyes were always sparkling. She was always smiling and had some encouraging words to say. It didn't matter if we talked about what the choir had just sung, a men's ministry activity I had coming up, or a fish Norm had caught that week. I always came away encouraged and blessed from having talked to Joyce.

One of the cards I received after her memorial service said, "Joyce Wright: Humble caregiver. Joy was a hero. She was a servant and was a joy to anyone who passed by her life. When I think about this lovely lady who now walks the streets of heaven I think of her entry to her celestial home—meeting her Savior who said, 'Well done, my faithful servant.'" This thought was reiterated by so many people.

Joyce also had an adventurous side, which came out whenever there was a disaster nearby. She was always ready to lend a hand and dig in to help those in need. She also enjoyed fishing—especially with me. She delighted in the simple pleasures and events of life and had a wonderful sense of humor.

Her love for Jesus Christ, her personal Savior, radiated around her. Her life was devoted to serving him in whatever way possible. She was an encourager of others and a woman of prayer. She reflected the influence of her godly mother, who was also a strong prayer. So often Joyce put aside her own needs and desires to minister to others. For almost 50 years she and her best friend, Fran, would pray together over the phone for family members, friends, and others in need. Joyce loved God's Word and shared what she learned with others.

I love Joyce. One day I'll say again, "Hello, Joyce."

H. Norman Wright

THE DISRUPTION OF
OUR LIFE TOGETHER

I do." Two words, that's all. But they signify the beginning of a committed relationship designed to last throughout life on earth. They are much anticipated words, and their expression to one another is filled with joy. Often they are said with a definite or emphatic tone because they're cementing the conclusion of the courtship journey and marking the entrance to the marital path.

Two little words...but very significant. Throughout the marriage there will be many couplets of words that become standard: "See you." "I'm home." "Food ready?" "What's up?" "Love you." "Let's go." "Ready yet?" These are all part of an ongoing relationship, and they connect two people together.

But there comes a time when words disconnect a relationship or signify with sadness it's over. As some words carry the feeling of joy or delight, others denote sorrow. When these are expressed they take the place of countless others now silenced and never to be heard again. Silence can be eerie, heavy, overwhelming. I heard it at "Ground Zero" in New York after the September 11, 2001 destruction. I heard it on the streets of destroyed homes in the Ninth Ward in New Orleans following Hurricane Katrina. Now I hear it every day in my home. There are words I'll never hear again from Joyce, and words I'll never say again to her. What I would give for one more conversation with her. Yes, I can put in a CD and hear Joyce's words. I can read again the letters I just discovered that she wrote to me during our courtship and the ones she wrote to her mother the first year of our marriage. But that's different. It's just not the same.

Now, in place of all the words of joy, there are others. "Goodbye" is a constant, whether I verbalize it or not. There is so much to say goodbye to. It seems endless. When something occurs I think of going home and sharing it with Joyce…but then certain words come to mind: "Not here." "Never again." The most difficult couplet occurs when someone asks how Joyce is or there's a phone call for her. I hesitate for a second before saying what I hate to: "Joyce died." I know it's necessary. I know it's true. But I wish it weren't. I still resist saying the words, but I force them out. It's reality.

So a new vocabulary centered around being alone has to be established.

The loss of our spouses changes our entire lives. It shifts the foundation of our existence. Nothing is as it was. Even the familiar becomes unfamiliar. Every aspect of our lives is disrupted without our partners. Everything has to be relearned, just as a flooded river does when it recedes and leaves behind a maze of new streams.

In a culture that doesn't like to acknowledge loss or talk about its impact, grieving is difficult. And when we add this silence to the fact that most of us have never been taught about the process and normalcy of grief, no wonder we struggle.

Prior to the death of your spouse, your life was going in a well-established direction. You had an identity. You could say who you were. This has changed. You're not exactly who you were. The person you lost was part of your identity. You were someone's spouse, someone's partner. You continue to be that person in your heart and memory, but there's a vacant place where your loved one stood.

Grief

We've probably all known grief to some degree. It can creep into our lives subtly and so slowly we're not always aware of its presence for a long time. There are some who have carried their grief for so many years they don't know anything else and believe that state to be normal.

Grief accompanies the slow deterioration of a spouse. Without even putting it into words you are grieving your mate's leaving you for weeks and months before he or she dies. That's what I experienced with Joyce. I knew…but I didn't want to know. I knew that it would soon be over when she said, "No more surgeries." I wouldn't allow myself to face the reality of the next few weeks…that there would be a time when Joyce would die. There was a part of me that said, "No! No, it won't happen." Even during the presence of people from hospice I denied it. "It can't happen. It won't happen to my Joyce. This isn't real."

Even today, after a month, there are times when I walk through the house sensing its emptiness but still saying, "No, she's not gone." If her absence is real that means the future, as well as the present, is one big "without." And the episodic bouts of intense grief are not just a gentle building of what was there before Joyce died, but more like an intruder that kicks the door down, comes in, and takes over.

Grief. What do you know about this experience? We use the word so easily. It's the state we're in when we've lost a loved one. It's an inward look. You've been called into the house of mourning. It's not a comfortable place. It's not where you want to reside, but for a time, longer than you wish, you will. Often it will hurt, confuse, upset, and frighten you. Grief can be described as intense emotional suffering and acute sorrow.

In grief the bottom falls out of your world, especially when a spouse is lost. The solid footing you had before is gone. The floorboards are tilting or turning into soft, pliable mud with each step you take. The stability of yesterday's emotions gives way to feelings that are so raw and fragile you think you're losing your mind. You're alone. Well, you *feel* alone, but you're really not. Jesus is with you. He's "a man of sorrows, acquainted with bitterest grief" (Isaiah 53:3 TLB).

Grieving is a very disorderly process. You have no control over it, and you can't schedule every aspect of its expression. People live according to schedules. So when you've experienced a major loss you're really thrown. Grief knows no schedule. It won't fit into your appointment book.[1] It's like an invader from another planet as it disrupts your mind and your thinking ability. Perhaps your mind is stuck on your last conversation with your husband or wife.

The author of *Healing After Loss,* Martha Hickman, said,

> Now there are spaces in the mind, spaces in the days and night. Often, when we least expect it, the pain and the pre-occupation come back and back—sometimes like the toiling crash of an ocean wave, sometimes like the slow ooze after a piece of driftwood is lifted and water and sand rise to claim their own once more.[2]

Your Reflections

1. Describe your grief during the first month.

2. Describe how your grief is now.

2

THE ONSLAUGHT OF GRIEF

It happened again. Grief hit…but not subtle, gentle, or gradual this time. It was a sudden, intense onslaught, viciously slapping my peace and calm out of the way. Perhaps it was so intense because of the stable calm that existed prior to its entrance. Thanksgiving actually went well with family and friends. It was after I got home that the reality of my present and future life was confronted again. I opened a packet I received in the mail. It contained the papers I needed to sign to roll a retirement IRA for Joyce over into mine. Just seeing her name printed there and realizing what I was signing was all it took. The last straw was the statement that I needed to send in an original death certificate with this set of papers.

The next day I received a call from the store where I was having a collage of seven or eight pictures of Joyce put together and framed. I was anticipating receiving this finished product to place on my wall. What I wasn't expecting was my response when I went to the store and the person at the counter removed the covering and showed me the display. I had no warning. And I'm not sure I even focused on or saw all the pictures, but I saw enough to feel overwhelmed. It's as though this collage had a message for me: "Joyce is gone. She died. She's no longer here. You're alone…and it's final."

I fell apart. I couldn't really think for several seconds, and I didn't know what to do or say when my mind turned back on. Grief slammed into my side and totally disrupted and disconnected me from a sense of stability. In retrospect, I'm not surprised grief did this, for I know it well. It was the suddenness and the way I was blindsided. Yes, it's happened before, and I know it will again. Can you relate?

Sometimes in your grief you may feel you're on a crooked sidewalk, being pushed along without being able to stop, look around, get your bearings, or even decide whether this is the direction you want to go. Grief brings you into the world of the unknown.

You may find yourself easily distracted and perhaps disoriented, even if you're normally a decisive person. You may discover you're now afraid to make choices. You feel childlike. During the next few months, decisions have to be made. It's not the best time of your life for any choices because of your emotional wounds. But some can't be delayed. Financial considerations, living arrangements, and family concerns may not be avoidable at this time. Major decisions during the first year of grief will be flavored by intense emotions. Some people will urge you to make a decision one way and others encourage the opposite. Take your time. Don't be rushed. Ask God to give you a clear mind and lead you to decisions or to those who have your best interests at heart.

Your Reflections

1. What have been the greatest surprises in your grief experience?

2. What decisions are you struggling with at this time?

3. Who are the people you can trust that have your best interests at heart?

3

TIME AND YOUR FUTURE

You may find that your sense of time is distorted. Time goes too fast or too slow. One morning I wrote:

My Journal

Time. There are days when I would like to sit down with "Time" and have a face-to-face discussion were it possible. I think I'd like to ask it some questions like, "Why are you so slow some days? You seem to drag at the time I need you to speed up and move on. Can't you accelerate the grief process? I'd like it to break the sound barrier, but it seems stuck in low gear." Some days it seems the day will never end. Sleep has become a welcome respite and retreat. Yes, I dream, and once in a great while I dream about Joyce. My dreams have always been vivid and active, but so far grief hasn't penetrated their themes. Perhaps it will, but for now the dreams are welcomed. The early mornings with all my chores and activities are all right as long as my mind doesn't access certain images and memories.

The past and future seem to collapse together. The future is hard to fathom. Some people shut out both the past and the future, but to survive and recover we need the memories *and* hope. There is wisdom in this thought: "Reminiscing is intended to liberate you from emotional claims of the past in order to think hopefully about the future." Are you wondering if there is a future? I did.

A Vague Future

The future has changed. We tend to believe it's never ending. It will go on forever...or so we assume. But grief drops a curtain over that belief. It's difficult to imagine the future when you're trapped in a fog. To envision a future you need to make some forward progress and avoid being permanently stuck in a quagmire. The clarity and anticipation of a future has faded into uncertainty. The dreams you once had included a companion at your side...and now there's just an empty space. Your mind tells you many messages: "He (or she) is with the Lord, and you'll be all right." "The future is still there and bright." "You will heal in time." "You can do it." But your heart says something different and grief short-circuits your mind and heart's attempts to work together.

Perhaps we say, "The future? Yes, but what kind? What will it be like?" And yet we direct little energy toward considering the future since it is evasive and painful to contemplate because of the empty space within its image.

When we lose a loved one, almost everything in us and around us changes at the moment of the death. Or it seems to. We feel isolated. And we may feel the world is now a vast, confusing, and chaotic place. We long for just a few moments with our loved ones. We reflect on the happiness our mates brought into our lives. Nothing else makes sense to us because the rare and meaningful relationships we cherished are now gone. Consumed by our devastating losses and our longings, we see ourselves and the world much differently than we ever have before. *From this time on,* we think, *the world will never be the same.* And in a very real sense, our world *was* changed the moment our loved ones died. Each person we love makes up a precious and vital piece of our world. At such a challenging time, we need to be patient with the chaos we are now enduring inside us and around us.[1]

Your Reflections

1. In what ways has your sense of time been impacted?

2. What are your thoughts about the future?

4

AM I NORMAL?

Have you wondered about and questioned your sanity? If you're experiencing intense grief, the "crazy" feelings are actually a *sane* response! The following examples are all symptoms of *normal* grief.

- distorted thinking patterns
- "crazy" or irrational thoughts
- fearful thoughts
- feelings of despair and hopelessness
- out of control or numbed emotions
- changes in sensory perceptions (sight, taste, smell, etc.)
- increased irritability
- want to talk a lot or not at all
- memory lags and mental short circuits
- inability to concentrate
- obsessive focus on the loved one
- losing track of time
- increase or decrease of appetite and/or sexual desire
- difficulty falling or staying asleep
- dreams in which the deceased seems to visit
- nightmares with death themes
- physical illness such as flu and headaches
- shattered beliefs about life, the world, and God[1]

Your Reflections

1. Write an example by each one you've experienced and are experiencing now.

- distorted thinking patterns
  Before

  After

- "crazy" or irrational thoughts
  Before

  After

- fearful thoughts
  Before

  After

- feelings of despair and hopelessness
  Before

  After

- out of control or numbed emotions
  Before

  After

- changes in sensory perceptions (sight, taste, smell, etc.)
  Before

  After

- increased irritability
  Before

  After

- want to talk a lot or not at all
  Before

  After

- memory lags and mental short circuits
  Before

  After

- inability to concentrate
  Before

  After

- obsessive focus on the loved one
  Before

  After

- losing track of time
  Before

  After

- increase or decrease of appetite and/or sexual desire
  Before

  After

- difficulty falling or staying asleep
  Before

  After

- dreams in which the deceased visits
  Before

  After

- nightmares with death themes
  Before

  After

- physical illness such as flu and headaches
  Before

  After

- shattered beliefs about life, the world, and God
  Before

  After

All this is normal! You certainly don't need to be "fixed." You're not broken. Your grief will take longer than you think, and it tends to intensify at three months, on special dates, and at the one-year anniversary of your partner's death.

If you find yourself struggling with sleep, you may find it beneficial to read these passages from the Scriptures out loud prior to closing your eyes. They will help.

When you lie down, you will not be afraid; when you lie down your sleep will be sweet (Proverbs 3:24).

You can sleep without fear; you need not be afraid of disaster or the plots of wicked men, for the Lord is with you; he protects you (Proverbs 3:24-26 TLB).

I lie awake at night thinking of you—of how much you have helped me—and how I rejoice through the night beneath the protecting shadow of your wings (Psalm 63:6-7 TLB).

Lord, when doubts fill my mind, when my heart is in turmoil, quiet me and give me renewed hope and cheer (Psalm 94:19 TLB).

I will lie down and sleep in peace, for you alone, O LORD, make me dwell in safety (Psalm 4:8).

5

THE OTHER ANNIVERSARIES

Sometimes it's the other anniversaries that overwhelm us: The last day you spoke or had a special date or your engagement day or... It helps to anticipate these as much as possible and mark your calendar. And then there are the holidays.

My Journal

Thanksgiving. It's here. The first holiday alone, and what it will bring I have no idea. As I write, my emotions are flat...very little feeling but many thoughts. It's a day of celebration, but without one of the celebrants. It's a day to be thankful, but it's marred by an absence, which inserts sadness as an underlying garment and dampens the entire day. Whether it's visible or not, there will be an empty chair at the table. Perhaps it would be better if we actually set an extra chair at the table to designate "missing one," like they do in a squadron of jets flying over a memorial service. They keep an empty position in their formation.

Sometimes it feels as though there's an empty chair strapped to my side wherever I go. It's not always conscious but it does break through as a reminder, "You're going there alone, by yourself, this time and forever." But I must participate in holidays and other events if I am to move on. I don't like it, but I must.

My Journal

Christmas Day, 2007. A day I knew would finally arrive. It's quiet on the streets, very few are out and around. Families and couples are clustered together, probably taking a break from foraging through all the gifts and getting a second wind for the annual feast.

My family had our gift opening. I think Sheryl [my daughter] was stunned when she received a package from Joyce. Her facial expression revealed she was overwhelmed. The "Mother's Book of Memories" took her breath away.

I'd forgotten that at one time Sheryl said she wished Joyce had left her something in writing. She did, but she never got it completed. She started this book in 2001, finishing about a fourth of it. At that point she started writing entries in snatches on pieces of paper. She wanted to complete this project and hoped to…but her cancer diverted many of our dreams.

I spent the two weeks before Christmas gathering letters, poems, and anything I could find of Joyce's and her mom's writings to inscribe in this book. It was a more difficult task emotionally than I realized it would be, but it was so worthwhile for Sheryl and me.

Sheryl's opening of this gift and our looking through its pages together set us off on a grief roller coaster, to say the least.

Returning home and cooking a duck and a pie was a diversion from the hollowness of this day. Like other days and experiences, Christmas is the best of times with friends last night and today…but also the worst. It's a time of remembering the past and experiencing the blessings of the present. Perhaps the most difficult was the message on the telephone answering machine from a friend who must not have heard the news about Joyce: "I just wanted to wish you and Joyce a blessed Christmas." And more than anything I wished it were true. That Joyce was by my side listening. I stood in silence as I hung up the phone.

Your Reflections

1. What are your experiences so far with anniversaries and holidays?

2. What special days are coming up in the next six months? How will you prepare for them?

6

Caution—Fragile

Some grieving spouses try to get others to carry their burdens. But grief can't be shared. Everyone has to carry his or her own. You'll vacillate between being emotionally fragile to being in an emotional coma. The grief you're experiencing is a demanding and overpowering intruder. It's all-consuming and disruptive, leaving holes and confusion in your life. It's reasonable that your responses to life and to others at this time will be unreasonable at times. You're in a state of exhaustion. At first you may feel like you're experiencing an internal emotional hemorrhage. Because of the severe loss, your focus needs to be on yourself. You need to treat yourself as if you were in intensive care. Why? Because you are emotionally vulnerable, exhausted, and weak.[1]

Grief involves a multitude of concepts. Let's look at some of them, beginning with "without" in this chapter.

Without. There was a time when your world consisted of you and your spouse. You probably didn't realize just how much he or she was "your" life, but now you're aware all too much. There's a hole in your personal life, as well as in your daily routine and schedule. You may not be fully aware of just how much has changed until you realize that now everything seems to involve living and doing "without" your spouse. Now you feel alone.

In marriage we develop a lifestyle of "we" and a sense that this is the way it will always be. Joyce and I experienced this. We were a couple for 48 years. We chose togetherness. But with death came absence, and now aloneness becomes the great disruption. Her presence is no more. The comfortable has slid like an icy avalanche into discomfort and unacceptable pain. This is not a choice. It's forced on us.

All the activities that were shared together must now be done in isolation—or at least it feels that way. What was shared can now only be shared in memory, and we enter into the world of "without." Everywhere I turn I'm without Joyce. It's as though I entered a train station with two different sets of tracks and a train on each one. Most engines have names as did these two. One is named "Without" and the other is "Blessings." At this time the "without" train is raging and has a full head of steam, ready to move in a second. The "blessings" train is sitting quietly. Every now and then it may let out a tiny puff of steam, but the other train is the one that forges ahead.

Someday…one day…the "without" train and its energy will begin to diminish. Its wheels will slow and its momentum will fade. Slowly, ever so slowly, it will fall behind its counterpart and eventually the "blessings" train will catch up with and pass the "without" train. The past will become a distant speck.

Once in a while "without" may forge ahead again, but it can't sustain its former pace. For some reason it has to make its presence known. Perhaps it comes because some of the memories have dimmed and there's a subconscious fear of forgetting the one who was loved. The train's momentum is a cry to the memory of the loved one: "See, you haven't been forgotten…and you never will be!" And then the "without" train falls behind again. And perhaps someday its wheels will slow even more, even grinding to a stop. A great sigh will come from the engine as it rests. "Without" has accepted you're moving on in life. Its presence is no longer because someday "without" will be replaced by "together" again.

Your Reflections

1. Describe your feelings of "without" at this time.

2. What comforts you the most right now?

Losses

When you lose your spouse, what you're missing is more than the presence of another person. You have what are called "secondary losses." They can include:

bill payer

business partner

checkbook balancer

companion

confidante

cook

counselor

couple friends

dreams of the future

encourager

errand person

friend

gardener

handyman

inspiration and insights

laundry person

lover

mechanic

memory sharer

mentor

motivator

organizer

prayer partner

protector

provider

sports partner

tax preparer

teacher

the world you knew

Your Reflections

1. What other things did your spouse do or did the two of you do together that you no longer do?

2. Take a look at these words and definitions. Then identify which ones you identify with the most. Note when they usually occur and how you handle them.

- *Amputation*—It feels as though part of you has been amputated, but you aren't sure which part is missing.

- *Longing*—There is a yearning within your heart and mind for your spouse to return.

- *Apathy*—You don't care about what you used to care about, and you have little or no energy for anything.

- *Yearning*—The desire persists for many things now lost to you, including undoing anything you have regrets about (such as things said or not said) and the death.

- *Ache*—The experience is worse than an ache. Your entire being is suffering since your body and mind are grieving.

Sometimes what we miss isn't tangible. It could be sounds or the sense that we're not alone. Sometimes what we miss causes us to think and to change and to grow. That's happened with me. This is what I experienced one day. With the pain of emptiness and the thought of my own journey to heaven came gratitude.

My Journal

Questions of life…and death. Once again I'm missing something. The house is quiet. It's pleasant. It's warm. It's comfortable. But it's empty. I'm here, as are the cats and the dog. But so often we look at one another, and all we hear is silence. There used to be chatter, soft as it was. There were sounds coming from everywhere Joyce was because she enjoyed talking and processing out loud. How many times did I ask, "Are you talking to me?" only to hear, "No, just to myself"?

I can hear Joyce's voice and remember some of her words. The delight of what we saw and experienced in the Tetons when she would see some wild animal and say, "Oh, stop…stop! Back up and go down this road. We can get closer and you can take a picture!" (To add to the hundreds we already had of moose and elk.) Her eyes were always alert and scanning for something interesting. When we drove she would see something of interest and I can still hear her voice, "Oh look—look at that!" And I would respond with "I can't! I'm driving."

And there are the times she would talk to our son, Matthew, in a soft, loving manner. Her "I love you" and "thank you for praying" words will be with me forever.

But so will other words that will echo forever in my memory. The five bravest words I've ever heard were uttered by Joyce on a fateful afternoon in the oncologist's office: "How long do I have?" Five simple words at the end of a sentence that started with, "If I decide not to have any more surgeries, how long do I have?" Isn't this what we all wonder?

Don't we all want to know that we're going to live to be a hundred, be in good health, and remain free from pain and suffering? We want to know but we don't want to really know because we're afraid we won't like the answer. It's never enough time. It's too soon…too short. The answer will change our lives, take away our hopes, and place a heaviness over the rest of our days.

I wonder, *Could I have asked the questions Joyce asked?* I don't know; I'm not sure. I think Joyce knew it wasn't long. It's one thing to sense death and even deny it, but it's another to ask what you've been wondering and then listening to what you've been afraid to hear. At least it would be for me. I don't know what Joyce thought at that moment. I know I didn't want to hear the answer. I felt like I was shrinking into the chair. That life had come to a halt, and time was standing still. A jail door had just slammed shut. The sentence had been pronounced and soon would be carried out.

"How long do I have?" Do we really want to know? Most of us don't. It's an erosion of hope that puts a damper on our future. In fact, it taints the present too. The answer Joyce received stole her future. It shattered my future, as well as our daughter's and granddaughter's.

I wonder what went through Joyce's mind when she heard, "It could be two weeks or even two months"? Was there despair or relief? Lingering hope laced with denial? Or a "That's what I thought"?

She asked the question, heard the news, and then needed to make a life and death decision. With or without surgery, earthly existence was just a matter of finite time.

How would I respond? How would anyone respond?

Did the promises in God's Word flood her mind? Did she hear Jesus saying, "I go to prepare a place for you"?

We never have as long as we want, especially with the ones we love. We can't really imagine how painful emptiness can be. And so there is a tension, a struggle, between focusing on the present pain of daily living and the reminder that death is just a transition. There will be a reunion! Joyce went first, and someday I'll catch up. She set the example by facing the reality of death, by being willing to hear the message "not long at all" and making peace with it by saying, "No more surgery."

How long do I have? How long do any of us have? Less time than we think or want. May we make every moment count for God's glory and his kingdom.

My Journal

Thank you, Joyce, for those five words, "How long do I have?" Thank you for showing me what courage really is and helping me understand. I love you.

8

WHY?

When the death first occurs there may be a sense of disbelief that causes you to see everything as if you're looking through a veil or a gauze curtain. Nothing is sharp or in focus. You may be asking "Why?" countless times a day. You may be shouting and shaking your fist. Or you may not be asking "Why?" Either way is all right. You may wonder, *Do I have the right to ask why?* You wonder if God will be upset if you question what happened. It's human to ask. Job asked this question 16 times. "Why?" is not just a question—it's also a heart-wrenching cry of protest, of pain. It means "No! This shouldn't be! It isn't right!" Others have asked too:

> Why, O LORD, do you stand far off? Why do you hide yourself in times of trouble? (Psalm 10:1).
>
> How long, O LORD? Will you forget me forever? How long will you hide your face from me? How long must I wrestle with my thoughts and every day have sorrow in my heart? How long will my enemy triumph over me? (Psalm 13:1-2).

Even Jesus asked!

> My God, my God, why have you forsaken me? (Matthew 27:45).

"Why?" is saying "I need some explanations. I need some answers." And receiving no answer can feed our anger. This brings up a side question to this issue. Would any answer suffice at this time? Is there any answer that would ease your heart? More than likely the answer is "No, not really." Answers don't always make pain go away. But even if there are no answers, it's okay to ask. Don't let others keep you from voicing your pain. And don't be offended by their answers or their lack of understanding. They probably are just trying to help you in a very difficult and awkward situation.

No Answers

One of the greatest feats of life is learning to live without answers. Our "Why?" questions form on our lips soon after we learn the word as a small child. And we continue asking as we search for answers and meaning in our lives. But most of the time when we engage in the whispered or even shouted "Why?" we end up in a monologue rather than a dialogue. When we ask we often believe an answer will give satisfaction to our yearning and pain. But can a simple explanation put our struggle to rest and calm our discomfort? Not always. The reality is we may experience even greater discomfort with a response.

"Why?" is expressed in subtle forms as well: "I wonder if…" "Could it be…" "What was going on behind those vacant, staring eyes?" The constant questions can perpetuate our pain and overshadow the normal events of our days. We may even miss what God is doing in and through our lives. Unanswerable life questions can keep us swirling in a whirlpool of turbulence. But like a journey down a river, troublesome rapids eventually lead to a stretch of calm…and the pattern continues until we exit the raft.

We can't demand answers to our questions. We can ask—and it's part of our nature to ask. But ultimately we must depend on and trust in God. We need to remember who we are and who God is. And could it possibly be that within the "no answer" there exists the mercy and comfort of God? Yes. He knows what we can know, what we can understand, and what we can handle. His answer to our painful "Why?" is, "I know it hurts. I know it doesn't make sense to you. I know that living 'without' is not what you want. Trust me. Rely on me. I love you. Someday…someday you won't need your questions."

I encourage you to keep asking when you need to. In time a transformation will occur as you let God into your pain. One day your "Why?" will turn into "What can I do to grow through this experience?" and "How will my life be stronger now?" Faith is involved in the process. On one hand you will ask why and on the other hand you will say, "I will *learn* to live by faith." Faith is many things. It is not knowing the answer and being willing to wait for God's reply. Eventually you may say, "I really don't need the answer to go on." Some say not knowing makes recovery difficult, but maybe knowing would make life even more difficult. We hope an explanation will lessen the hurt, but that's not always going to happen.

Your Reflections

1. What questions have you asked?

2. What would you like to ask?

9

WHY GRIEF?

Why do we have to go through grief? What is the purpose? Grief is about basically four things:

1. Through grief you express your feelings about your loss. And you invite others to walk through it with you.

2. Through grief you express your protest at the loss as well as your desire to change what happened.

3. Through grief you express the effects you have experienced from the devastating impact of the loss.

4. Through grief you may experience God in a new way that will change your life. Job said, "My ears had heard of you but now my eyes have seen you" (Job 42:5).

Along this difficult journey we will probably experience what's called "grief spasms." An intense upsurge of grief happens suddenly and when least expected. It's disruptive, and we will feel out of control. Some describe it as continuing waves of painful grief. And it doesn't take much to cause this to occur. Some refer to it as being "ambushed by grief."

Blindsided

One Sunday afternoon I was watching a football game. A receiver went downfield, turned around, and caught a pass. He never saw the linebacker who hit him from behind and knocked him back three yards. The receiver was blindsided. I've felt that way. At our church we have a "Remembrance Service" just before Christmas for anyone who has lost a loved one within the last two or three years. This is a time of reflection. My friend Rex and I arrived early and went into the foyer. We stood at the sanctuary entrance and listened to two women rehearsing their duet. I didn't want to be at this service. But there I was. And then it hit. I was blindsided by the most intense grief surge I've ever experienced. It moved through my body, and I walked away almost trembling. My sobs were inaudible but there. After that I carried a low-grade grief fever for a day or two. Balance finally returned.

Because I'm a counselor by profession, many have asked me, "What about your grief? What do you do with it when you're out assisting others?" Ministering and helping others is part of my healing process. It's important to reinvest in others. Recently I went to Colorado Springs to assist a church following a shooting. Even as I traveled there, my mind occasionally went back to images and thoughts of Joyce. But I stayed in work mode and told myself, *No, not now. Not at this time.* I knew the effect grief could have on me. Maybe there would be an occasion before returning home that I could relax and let go a bit. This I could control to some extent. (There were other situations and triggers that I had no control over whatsoever.) I'm always aware of the grief. It's lurking under the surface like giant bass waiting for an opportunity to engage in a feeding frenzy.

When I'm out teaching or counseling, there are usually a few times when grief breaks through. I come close to a meltdown, but I realize that my focus needs to be on others so I usually manage to put it off until I can unravel in private. I'm aware that it's coming in the next few days following a ministry and this is all right. It needs to. Often, as I get close to home, I begin to feel different. Grief creeps up on me emotionally, like when I'm lying in bed and I'm cold and I slowly and gently pull a blanket up over me.

Occasionally as I go about my day I'll feel the grief moving about, looking for an opening to surge through. Perhaps the more I restrict it the more energy it gains. As I write this it seems silent, as though sleeping, but I know it will awaken. When? Only grief knows for sure.

After I returned home from my trip to Colorado, the sadness came and went. And I was fine. I was "without," but okay.

As we reside in a world characterized by "without"—without the ones we loved in every aspect of our lives—we feel pain. We need to relearn who we will be "without" the other and how we will function. We need to relearn ourselves since when we lose someone we lose part of ourselves. We need to adjust our relationships with others and perhaps even with God, just as Job did. Remember, after his losses and trauma he cried out, "My ears had heard of you but now my eyes have seen you" (Job 42:5). Now we are relearning and reshaping our daily lives. We don't get *back* to normal, we create a *new* normal. We find our way to a purposeful, meaningful, and hopeful life again. We make choices for the present and the future to avoid becoming prisoners of the past. Yes, it's painful…and may take longer than you imagine.

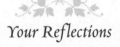

Your Reflections

1. Briefly describe the grief you've been experiencing.

10

EMPTY

Empty. There is an empty place in your life—a vacuum that nothing seems to fill. Unfortunately, it's necessary to become accustomed to the absence of someone who was a very important part of your life. In addition to experiencing the pain of the loss of your spouse, you have to adjust to the void left by your partner. The feeling of emptiness you experience will be directly related to how significant your spouse was in your life. Your task now is to figure out how to function without him or her. That's easier said than done.

My Journal

Something missing. I felt different yesterday. It was difficult to put my finger on how I felt. There were enough projects and errands and decisions to keep me busy. But I felt as though 90 percent of me was here and the rest was absent.

Many of the losses I feel are invisible. They have no form or substance or color, but they are real nevertheless. The feeling of "without" is like an amputation, except I can't point to what has been removed. I can't wrap my hands or heart around it.

In the afternoon I came inside the house, and it felt like there was a void. Something that should have been there, that rightfully belonged there, wasn't. Something was missing. Joyce was missing. Suddenly I missed Joyce with an intensity I'd never experienced before. And like lava surging to the surface of a mountainous volcano, sobs and tears erupted and wouldn't stop. They were so intense that for the first time my dog, Shadow, came from the other room to see what was wrong. Nothing new had happened. I was just different now, and he was bothered. But hugging and holding him calmed the both of us. His quiet and loving presence was soothing. The exhaustion that comes after such an upheaval helped me sleep that night.

In losing your loved one, you've suffered a great loss. Eventually you have to learn to move on without that special relationship. Living is about coping and growing. You turn over in bed to put your arm around your spouse, and the reality hits again that he or she is no longer part of your life.

You have to adjust to function without the interaction and validation you were accustomed to receiving from him or her. The lack of your loved one's presence in your life means many things. Your needs, hopes, dreams, expectations, feelings, and thoughts are forced to change. Slowly over time, the reality of separation sinks in, and you realize, "For now, I exist without my partner. I'm living without my mate." You live "without." I'm still feeling the discomfort of this condition.

Your Reflections

1. Describe what you miss the most at this time.

2. What's the most difficult step in moving on in your life?

NO LONGER HERE

Every time you get excited or when something goes wrong, you rush to tell your spouse...only to discover again that he or she is *no longer here*. It's a fact, and there will be many reminders. You won't be able to do or say much of what you used to.

My Journal

What I used to say... There are phrases I used to say that are no longer a valid part of my vocabulary. It's strange how often phrases become a habitual major part of a relationship. Sometimes we think about what we'll say and other times it comes from countless repetitions.

"Joyce, where are you?" "I'm home!" "How ya doing?" "What's for dinner?" "Any calls?" "Did you talk to Sheryl today?" "Shadow, take the paper into Joyce." "I love you." "Can I get you anything?"

Phrases are dropped throughout our lives as friends and relatives pass on. "Did Mom call?" "How's your mom doing?" "Did you talk to the home to see how Matt is doing?"

Sometimes I catch myself starting to say one of these phrases and wishing so much that it would be possible again, that Joyce is here and will respond with "I'm in here." "I'm all right." "It's good to see you." "Here are your calls. Fran called. Your brother called." "I love you too." "Good dog to bring me the paper."

I still hear these in my mind. In time they too will fade. Another "without." Another void. Another loss.

Survival Mode

How do we deal with this void? What can we do? Broaden our roles and our skills and learn to function without our mates. We'll learn to make up for what we lost. We change what we do and take on the responsibilities our spouse handled. There will be some things we give up, that we choose not to do anymore. Adjustment means not behaving the same way we did when our partners were active parts of our world.

For many, the loss of a spouse means acquiring a new identity. You will never be quite the same as you were before the loss. As one person said, "That portion of my life is history. I will never be that way or be that person again." You won't do or say what you used to, and sometimes the inability to do this hurts.

Look at the people around you and think about how losses were probably turning points in their lives. Often people point to the time of change as a time of new direction. My mother, who died at 93, lost her first husband when she was 34. When she was 61, her second husband (my father) was killed in an automobile accident. Major changes in her life occurred after each of these events. When a spouse dies we're no longer a husband or wife. We're a widower or widow. And we don't like those words.

Perhaps the most crucial task to be completed now is developing a new relationship with the one you lost, and that's not something we want to do or know how to do readily.

Your Reflections

1. In what ways can you develop a new relationship with your departed spouse?

12

ALIVE IN YOUR MEMORY

Developing a new relationship involves keeping your spouse alive in your memory in a healthy and appropriate manner. Formation of a new identity *without* his or her presence is another step that needs to be completed. Again that word "without"! Hang on to every memory you can. They're special.

The Gift of Memories

One of the experiences that activate my longing for Joyce's presence, as well as that empty feeling and intense sadness, is picturing her sitting on the couch one day during the last month of her life.

My Journal

I came down the hall after having been out for a while. Joyce had her back to me, and when she heard me she stood and turned around. With a smile and look of simple pleasure on her face, she said, "Oh, I just wanted to see your face." It was one of those greetings of unrestricted delight and acceptance that let me know all is well in spite of the circumstances. To know that seeing me again was so important to her was a wonderful gift to me. It's not like other gifts that I can pick up and hold and continue to savor its presence. That's why I feel compelled to write about it now. In time, this description I'm composing will be all I have left.

Our memories have a built-in fade mechanism over which we have little control. As important as some images are, the ones we want to keep will diminish. Have you noticed that? The images we want to eliminate tend to be tenacious in their ability to linger and resist our attempts at eviction. The memories we long to hang on to seem to fade much too quickly. That's why photos and other keepsakes of our loved ones are so valuable. There's a photo of Joyce I want to keep forever. She was out with some friends for her birthday, and the photo captures the sweet expression of the moment.

One way to develop a new relationship as well as honoring your spouse is to create a "memory book." Capture your thoughts, feelings, and memories about him or her in a scrapbook that includes written descriptions, visual reminders, and photographs of his or her life. Unlike more open-ended journals of expressive writing that focus more on your private experience, memory books typically represent what can be more easily shared with or even compiled by multiple individuals. In a sense they represent an extension of a birth or wedding album, but with a focus on the last of life's transitions.

Some of the statements to use are:

• My first memory of you was...

• My favorite times with you were...

• What I love most about you is...

• What others say about you is...

• Your favorite activities were...

• Your favorite words of wisdom were...

• When I think of you, I...

• I keep your memory alive by...

Be sure to have plenty of blank pages so you can adequately express what you want to.

Sometimes there is unfinished business in a relationship or unresolved difficulties. Rather than burying these problems, it's better to identify and face them so you can resolve them as much as possible. You can ask:

- What I most regret about our relationship is...
- What I never heard you say was...
- What I wish you could hear is...
- You most disappointed me when...
- My most troubling memory of you was when...
- I know that I am moving ahead when...[1]

As you move on, the emotional energy that was once invested in your spouse becomes freer and you start reinvesting in other people, activities, and hopes that can, in turn, give you emotional satisfaction. At first I did this through ministering to others in seminars I conducted and counseling others.

Your Reflections

1. Write down some thoughts based on the questions in this chapter that will help you get started on creating a memory book.

2. Write down some thoughts that will help you begin to resolve any leftover issues you have regarding your marriage.

13

A New Relationship

How do you develop a new way of relating to the one you lost? Death ends the person's life but not your relationship. This isn't morbid or pathological. It's perfectly normal. But few talk about it. Have you heard a discussion about such a relationship as being normal? Probably not. And if you bring it up for discussion, people might worry that you've gone over the edge. If people tell you that the best way to deal with your loss is to forget the person or not think about him or her, they're blocking your grief experience. Don't listen to them.

We keep people alive all the time. We reflect on who they were, what their achievements were, and how they impacted society. I've heard a number of people make the statement, "I wonder what he would think if he were alive today?" or "Wouldn't she be surprised to see all of this?" People contemplate what their deceased spouses would do in certain situations, using memories of what the person would do as one of several options.

What's abnormal is if you feel you must do things or see things just the way your spouse did. You don't. You can choose.

Sometimes when we lose someone who has played a significant part in our lives, our memories of them become distorted. With the loss of a spouse, the usual response is to recall only the positive aspects. But in time, there must be realism. Thoughts and memories need to be reviewed realistically to include the good and the bad, the positive and the negative. We need to remember the situations we're glad occurred *and* those we wish hadn't happened. By doing this, a balanced, accurate pool of memories develops. This is what's needed to develop the new relationship with your spouse. This realistic view will generate accompanying feelings as you face the realization that the person is no longer with you.[1]

At some point in time, it may be helpful to write a relationship history graph about your partner and identify the positives and negatives of your relationship. (A sample graph is on the next page.)

On the bottom portion of the graph, positive events and experiences are listed. I suggest you list 5 to 15 separate events. On the top part of the line, negative, upsetting, or hurtful experiences are identified.

On completing this, you may find that other significant events come to mind. Add them as they come to mind. Now write a list or paragraph for each event, giving as much description as possible (positive and negative).

It's important to allow *all* your feelings to emerge. Some of them may come under the category of "if onlys" or "regrets." Take the time to list these too. These could pertain to both positive and negative experiences. Your list may look something like this:

- Midlife crisis—My feelings are all mixed up. I wish they were clearer.
- I'll never forget the times we prayed together. They meant so much.
- I'm glad we have pictures and videos from our anniversaries.
- I'm still hurt over the drinking. I wish it hadn't been part of our marriage.
- I'm sorry for my angry outbursts.
- I'm angry you died so young. I feel cheated. Our marriage was getting better when you died. We needed more time.
- I wish we could have talked more. There's so much more I wanted to tell you.

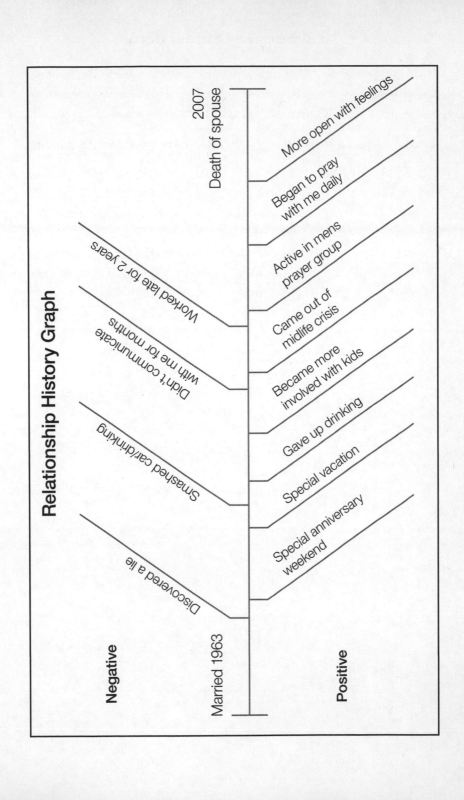

Your Reflections

1. Make a preliminary list to get you started on your relationship history.

   •

   •

   •

   •

   •

   •

   •

   •

   •

   •

   •

14

Never Enough

Some of the statements in the last chapter may bring to mind such thoughts as: *I wish things could have been different. I wish things had been better. I wish we had spent more time together,* and *I wonder what would have happened if...* These reflect our critical attitude toward what we did or didn't do and what the deceased person did or didn't do. If we remain in this critical stage, inaccurate memories of the relationship emerge. And the more this happens, the more difficult it is to complete our grieving. I went through a difficult time of this. My daughter and a friend read a rough draft of this chapter and, fortunately, verbally slapped me back to reality, letting me know Joyce knew I loved her.

My Journal

Did We Do Enough?

In life the phrase "never enough" resides in most of us. Some would admit to it whereas others deny its presence. Who wouldn't want more of whatever brings satisfaction or delight to our lives. For some it's a constant nagging sense of dissatisfaction that diminishes the benefit of what they have received, while for others it's because what they experienced was so wonderful they want it to continue if possible.

Parents are heard to tell their children, "You're never satisfied."

Spouses are heard to tell their partners, "You're never satisfied."

The "never enough" desire can create greed or generosity, selfishness or compassion.

We're admonished to have this feeling by what others have said to us. "You could have studied (practiced, worked out, listened, paid attention) more," and we incorporate their admonition into our belief system.

Sometimes we wonder if we couldn't have done more, if we really had done enough. We think, *I wonder...*

The movie *Saving Private Ryan* sent me down this pathway, and it's come back time to time over the past few months. In the movie a squad of soldiers are deployed to find a particular man in order to bring him home since his other brothers have already been killed. They eventually find him, but in the battles several of the searching soldiers are killed, including the captain. As the captain lies dying on a bridge and the battle has been won, he whispers to Private Ryan, "Earn this... earn this." And so Ryan goes through his life with these words ringing forever in the back of his mind: "Men died for you. Live up to their sacrifice for you. Don't let your life be wasted for it was bought by the blood of others." (How similar to our own redemption that was purchased by the blood of another—by Jesus Christ!)

At the conclusion of the film, Private Ryan is elderly and takes his family to Europe to visit the gravesite of his captain. His face reflects his memories as well as his feelings. His unspoken question is, *Did I earn this? Did I do enough? Could I have done more?* As his wife walks up to join him, he turns to her and asks with a sad, painful expression on his face, "Tell me I've led a good life. Tell me I'm a good man." Perhaps these were thoughts that haunted him over the decades. Maybe he asked himself these questions thousands of times like many of us do. But now he voiced them because he wanted to hear the affirmation, "You are."

Don't we all have questions about ourselves? About who we are, who we could be, what we could have done, and what we will be able to do? When a loved one dies, there are questions. Was I a good spouse? What could I have done differently? More of or less of? Sometimes these questions reflect just that—questions. In some cases they're evidence of regret or a wish that something could have been different or didn't occur at all.

I've heard some people say, "I have no regrets." Well, perhaps, but deep within us no matter how much we gave or did, we ask, "Did I really do enough? Could I have done more?"

I ask this. I wonder about many things. My actions may have been enough for me, but was it enough for Joyce? Did I do enough for her? Was it sufficient? Could I have done more or less in some areas? I wish I knew for sure, but I don't…and I never will.

And it's not just questions that arise about the last months of being together. No, they cover the entire marriage. In my case, it was more than 48 years of togetherness. *What did I forget to do? How did I disappoint her?* Some say these are futile questions because how can anyone formulate an answer that is factual rather than emotional? But perhaps that's why the question needs to be voiced, to be asked—to give words to the emotions we're feeling. The benefit is probably not in any answer but in the introspective process leading to the question.

And so I asked what more I could have done.

My Journal

- Was I attentive enough, Joyce?
- Did I listen to you enough?
- How could I have helped and supported you more in your times of confusion?
- Did I walk with you enough during the difficult days?
- Did I pray with you enough?
- Did I turn the radio up enough in the darkness of night so you could hear the music you loved?
- Did I encourage you enough in your uniqueness as a person?

- Did I encourage you enough in your art?
- How could I have helped you more with Matthew [our hand-icapped son]?

If we're too critical of ourselves, we tend to over-compliment the person who is no longer here. Perhaps you've heard someone talk about a deceased partner as if the person were a saint:

- "Why didn't I appreciate him more? He was so…"
- "I'll never find such a sensitive person again."
- "She was the perfect wife."
- "He was the perfect husband."

As you reflect on the "if onlys," regrets, and what you wanted better, different, or more of, what do you discover about your relationship? What events still need to be resolved? What you discover through this evaluation can bring you out of a pattern of denial and help you recover. The pain may seem too much and even unnecessary, but it's important for developing your new relationship.[1]

Your Reflections

1. What are your "if onlys"?

2. What are your "regrets"?

15

WHAT YOU REMEMBER

Is recalling how a loved one died necessary? Is it normal? The answer to both questions is yes. Repetitious reviewing helps you fully realize that your needs, hopes, expectations, and dreams of continuing to be with this person are *not* going to be fulfilled. You simply can't be with your spouse the way you used to be. Each time you review the death and surrounding events, your understanding of this will increase and perhaps more meaning will be added. You may tend to resist reflection since the memories bring pain, but each time you remember you'll discover you have more control.[1]

My Journal

Her pain was the greatest. Many have been so supportive and comforting before Joyce's death. The expressions of concern over what I was going through as a husband were many, but my attention was captured by what Joyce was experiencing.

She was the one with a stage-four tumor eating away at her brain.

She was the one who carried the burden for years of where this would end.

She was the one who searched for the elusive words to express her thoughts and feelings.

She was the one who thought she was saying something clearly but in reality she wasn't.

She was the one whose memory became distant and selective.

She was the one who lay in her bed with eyes closed, eyes open and staring, or with tears forming at the edges of her eyes.

This is the person of faith and courage for whom it was the most difficult.

My Journal

Not Afraid. Joyce was a woman of courage. She faced death and said, "I am not afraid." When confronted by the words, "If you have the surgery to remove this tumor, it will return again and sooner," she thought about it and asked, "If I decide not to go ahead with the surgery how long do I have?" She was told, "It could be two weeks or two months. But this is a decision you need to make for you, Joyce, not for anyone else. What do *you* want to do and what is best for you?" Although the surgery was scheduled, she thought and prayed about it. As was usual for her, she kept considering the needs of others. What would I want? What would our daughter, Sheryl, want?

Sheryl and I told her not to make her decision based on what we wanted, but on what she felt was best. As difficult as it was, we released her to a decision made between her and the Lord. And two days before her scheduled operation, and with a clear mind and speech, she said no to surgery and yes to heaven. The next night the pain increased, and the tumor began to bleed. Joyce went into a coma for ten days. And then death came.

Death took her from this life...but it launched her into eternal life with her Lord and Savior, Jesus.

Death took her from us—but not forever.

Death left a hole in our lives, but it made God's presence and comfort more real.

Death changed our lives. But out of the chaos I've developed a deeper faith and stronger hope for the future.

Your Reflections

1. What are your memories of the last day with your loved one?

2. Which memories do you want to remember? Which ones would you prefer to forget?

16

You're Still Alive

Each time I read what I've written in my journal I feel the pain of missing Joyce. I feel sad. But it is becoming easier. Some people never relinquish what they've lost. They hang on. They dwell on what they never had or what they lost, and it dominates their lives. Often they become bitter. And then there is the opposite reaction. Some act as though the other person never existed. They block his or her existence from their memory and attempt to move on. Neither of these approaches reflects a healthy response. There needs to be balance.

What are the healthy ways to handle having a deceased spouse and yet keep him or her alive in memory for you and others? This may sound strange, but the initial step is recognizing that the other person *is gone* and *you* are still alive. At first you may not feel as though you're very much alive. Sometimes people say they can't go on or don't want to go on without their spouses. But there does need to come a time of emotionally letting go and reinvesting in life in a new way.

Another step is deciding what there is about your life with the other person and your life together that can and should be retained. This includes deciding what is healthy. Do you continue to...

- go to the same coffee shop each morning for breakfast?
- go on an evening walk around the park?
- keep special items you either made or purchased together displayed?
- maintain any of the daily or weekly routines the two of you shared?[1]

Your Reflections

1. At this point, what do you do that you used to do together?

2. What have you purposely relinquished from your life with your partner?

Attending the monthly couples Bible study and potluck dinner might not be retained, even if people encourage you to come back "once in a while." It might be too painful for some people. Yet I have heard of others who continued in spite of the discomfort. In general, many of the couples' activities will probably be dropped.

Some healthy ways people relate to their deceased spouses may include...

- learning more about their favorite activities and involvements

- watching home movies or videos, listening to recordings of them, or reflecting on some of their stories to bring back memories of them

- deciding to try some of their favorite foods or engage in their former activities to experience what they did

Your Reflections

1. What could you do to relate in a new way?

17

MEMORIES OF DAYS PAST

Memories are preserved by visiting your childhood school, job sites, and special places. Years after my father died, I was able to find his original homestead in Maine and even locate some relatives. This brought back memories and expanded my knowledge of my father. It's also normal to talk about people we've lost, do things based on what we learned about them, and reflect on our memories.

Part of who you are today and how you respond is based on your relationship with your spouse. Perhaps he or she taught you new insights, perceptions, skills, appreciations, or values. Your mate left an indelible mark on you. Sometimes you may even be surprised as you discover yourself solving problems or responding in a manner he or she used to do.

My Journal

Memories of Lake Arrowhead. The memories hit the other day. They were intertwined with the images of what I was actually seeing as I drove through the mountains toward Lake Arrowhead. There were flashes of meals together at the Cliffhanger, where on a clear day we would gaze at Catalina or note on a rain-refreshed clear evening that the lights of the valley seemed to be on a continuous synchronized timer, blinking from bright to dim and on and off. And on some evenings we were sure the lights were on a plane headed right toward us so Joyce and I almost dove under the table. As I drove past the turnoff to Crestline, I remembered our first week of married life together spent in a small, inexpensive cabin where we learned to love and cook and fish together.

I found a treasure the other day. It was a letter you wrote to your mother the second day of our honeymoon. I really have no idea what you can see or hear or remember in heaven, but here's your letter.

Monday, August, 24, 1959—10:00 a.m.

Dear Mom and Pop,

This morning we're sitting out here on the beach getting tanned. It's beautiful weather here. Cool evenings and warm days. The trees and lake are very nice. Our cabin is really close to the market and lake. We've new plastic dishes and everything we need. Last nite we went to the evening service at a little Pres. church here. A new Baptist church is being built. We've been having a wonderful time doing nothing but loafing. Norm cooked breakfast this morning (burnt toast and bacon, runny eggs). But who cares, my husband is so wonderful!

Dad, Norm wants to thank you for our wedding. We both enjoyed it *so* much. It's something we'll never forget. We've still got our piece of cake in the middle of our table. We've frozen a piece to eat on our first anniversary.

My ears seem real fine. The altitude doesn't affect them.

Norm and I pray together every morning and evening. The Lord has blessed our lives together much more than we had ever hoped for.

It sure is getting nice and warm. We're going to rent a boat and fish. They're catching crappie, trout, and catfish here.

How do you like these notes, Mom? I'm sending the rest for you to use.

Lots of love,
Joy

I remember our walks in the forest, the time Dick Clark gave you a grocery cart in Jensen's market, when we saw Higgins of *Magnum PI* fame, the morning we launched our first boat in Lake Arrowhead and it snowed, the many dinners in the Royal Oak at Blue Jay with the same waitress. I saw her and discovered that her husband died last year. She remembered you (who could ever forget you!).

These are good memories. And that's all I have of you now. With the memories comes the ache, the longing, the thought of the future "without" and wondering…wondering about so many things.

Your Reflections

1. Friend, now you're on your own in so many ways, and in the midst of your pain you need to take on new roles and responsibilities, such as making decisions in new areas. Who was the primary decision-maker in your relationship? You, your spouse, or both? Reflect back on this important process for a moment.

Decisions my spouse made   Decisions I made Decisions made together

2. What are the most difficult everyday decisions you have to make now that your spouse is gone?

3. Now that you're alone, you'll have to make decisions that you perhaps never imagined you would have to make. What are those that need to be made in the next month?

4. What are those that need to be made in the next six months?

5. What are those that need to be made in the next three years?

18

Changing "We" to "I"

With the loss of your spouse, there is a change in identity from "we" to "I." This can be one of the most painful transitions of all. For instance, the first time I saw my name listed as "widower" I was taken aback. The world around you is seen differently. Some of your friendships may change as well. You will retain old ones, but adjustments have to be made. Your identity may have been as a couple, and most of your friendships are couple relationships. But now you're alone. Your time with couples will diminish. You will need to build new relationships with people who share portions of your new identity with you.

Moving on is reinvesting your emotional energy in something new that can give you satisfaction and fulfillment. The relationship with your spouse can't do this anymore. I'm not talking about a replacement. A new person is *not* a replacement for a former love, and any attempt to make him or her a replica is unhealthy. Instead of replacing, you can reinvest in a service organization, ministry, a new career, a new hope, and so on. Find a new direction for your life.

Your Reflections

1. What could you do now or in the future that's new?

19

What Your Loved One Wore

There are people who eliminate every visible vestige of their loved one just as soon as the funeral is over. Unlike those who keep all the reminders out and untouched, as if awaiting the loved one's return, these people believe they can shorten their grieving process by making their loved one vanish. Both extremes are unhealthy. People who dispose of every reminder, every memento, every article of clothing are bound to regret their actions later. It is far better to store your mate's possessions for a time until you can sort through them in peace and comfort.

My Journal

What she wore. It's been said that clothes make the person. It's also been said that the selection of what a person wears defines who a person is. I don't know if this is true or not. Some of us are more concerned with what we wear than others. There are those who grab the nearest article, while others make a careful selection based on where they are going. Joyce was very careful and attentive when it came to her selection of clothes. At times we would say as she came out in a new outfit, "Now, that's you…That's your outfit." It was rare indeed that she wore something that didn't reflect who she was. It's interesting that someone could coordinate her clothing with her personality as well as her character qualities, but Joyce did.

Perhaps that's why I've struggled so much the last two days. I felt it was time to disperse some of her winter clothing to a special group as they endeavored to reenter society. They need coats, warm sweaters, business suits, and shoes. I gathered these together, but it wasn't that easy. As I looked at many of the items I saw Joyce once again. It wasn't that a specific image came to mind but an impression, a sense that this was Joyce, and I've seen this on her before. A few that I looked at impacted me so much that I could hardly speak. I put those articles away to keep. The feelings and impressions came and left many times. At one point it seemed like a violation of Joyce, taking those items that caused others to remember her and giving them away to strangers. Expressed or not, it felt like I was saying, "Joyce has no need of these anymore. She's through with them. She's never coming back." The very act of sorting and dispensing becomes another reminder that a precious person is gone...has died. Sometimes even though we know it's reality, an act such as this is a painful reminder.

A major adjustment for anyone who has lost a spouse is what to do with the items left behind. One way of handling this is the pile plan. The purpose is twofold: to take charge of the remaining items so they don't overwhelm you, and to end up with what you really want to keep. It is often best to go through this procedure with another family member or close friend. Take all the items and make three piles. In one pile are those you are sure you want to give away. The second pile holds the items you want to keep for a while. The third pile contains the things you're not certain what to do with. Put these items in boxes and keep them until you're sure what you want to do with them.

This is not an easy task. It is not without pain. But our lives go on, different and new. How soon and how different and new depend on our personal grieving process.

My Journal

The closet. Closets are small, inconsequential parts of a house. We don't think much about them because they function as a storeroom, a place to put items when they're not in use. The clothes and garments are placed, residing until needed the next time. We pass by these repositories a dozen times a day or meander through them in search of an appropriate article. Sometimes the doors are left open, and on other occasions they're closed.

Joyce's closet door has been closed for several weeks. It's a storeroom of memories, a place filled with reflections of someone special. Once in a while I open the door, walk in, and gaze at what's hanging on the hooks or hangers. Some have wrappings on them from the cleaners and weren't worn again. Some were Joyce's favorites, and some were ones I enjoyed seeing her in. I touch some and smell others, hoping a bit of her fragrance remains. I can envision her in certain outfits for they reflect who she was—and still is in my mind. I resist the thought that she will never wear these clothes again. Joyce was careful about her appearance. She wanted to dress appropriately and properly, modest but in style, and with color combinations in which she was comfortable. Selecting the right outfit was never simple or easy. Just when I thought she had made her selection, I would return to the room and behold, she was dressed in a new outfit. And when she asked my opinion, she wanted more than "It looks fine" or "O.K." She needed elaboration and details. She was careful with clothes. In her case it wasn't that clothes made or enhanced the person but that she made or enhanced the clothes.

One day the door will remain open. I will select those items I want to remain with me and the others will be sent to help others. But not yet.

Your Reflections

1. What do you remember about your spouse's clothes?

2. What do you want to keep at this time?

20

REASONS FOR GRIEF

These were the two worst days so far. Emotional swings came often and then subsided after the eruption. I'm glad no one was around to hear me or they would have panicked. My dog, Shadow, and the cats have learned to accept my meltdowns. It wasn't that way with a close friend. He lost his son and wife in the last seven months. His breakdown came as he sat on a plane. He sobbed uncontrollably. That could happen to me. If so, it's all right, I suppose. My concern is not how this would affect others. Their discomfort is an opportunity for them to learn about grief. If not already, someday they too will experience its presence and pain.

We all search for reasons for our actions. When others hear about the last two days, will they wonder what set Norm off? Do I know? Perhaps...perhaps not. It could be the season. The music, the sights, the expectations, the driving and going places by myself while others are together, the comforting words on the cards or over the phone, the news that a friend lost his only child, a 14-year-old who had two heart transplants and then cancer. It could be ambling from room to room in the house several times a day searching and saying inaudibly, *Joyce, are you here? Where are you?* and hearing no response. I catch myself opening the closet door from time to time as if a glimpse of her clothes hanging on the hooks and rods or in a pile will say, "See, I'm still here." But it's not true. She *should* be here. She *ought* to be here. I want her here. But it's not to be nor will it ever be again on earth. So earth no, but heaven yes. Comforting to a degree, but eliminating the pain? No.

So if someone wants reasons for my difficult days, maybe this will suffice. At a time like this we don't need reasons for breakdowns. Rationality in the mind can never explain the responses of our hearts. Reasons don't make the situation better or more comfortable. The grief just has to happen, and it will happen with no boundaries of time or location allowed. It's just grief—plain old simple grief having its way for now. Can anything soothe? Oh yes, but only after grief has its way and spills out over everything and everyone. The Scriptures comfort and speak to our hearts and minds. Jeremiah, talking for God, said, "I will turn their mourning into joy, and I will comfort them and make them rejoice" (Jeremiah 31:13 TLB).

What do you need to know about suffering during his time?

- Your grief will take longer than most people think.

- Your grief will take more energy than you ever imagine.

- Your grief will involve many changes and will continue to develop.

- Your grief will show in all spheres of your life.

- Your grief will depend on how you perceive the loss.

- You will grieve for many things symbolic *and* tangible, not just for the death alone.

- You will grieve for what you have lost already, and for what you've lost for the future.

- Your grief will entail mourning, not only for the person you lost, but also for the hopes, dreams, and unfulfilled expectations you held for and with that person and for the unmet needs because of the death.

- Your grief will involve a wide variety of feelings and reactions—more than just the general ones often depicted, such as depression and sadness.

- Your loss will resurrect old issues, feelings, and unresolved conflicts from the past.

- You may have a combination of anger and depression, exhibited as irritability, frustration, annoyance, and intolerance.

- You will feel some anger and guilt—or at least some manifestation of these emotions.

- You may experience grief spasms—acute upsurges of grief that occur without warning.

- You will have trouble thinking about memories, handling organizational tasks, intellectually processing information, and making decisions.

- You may feel like you're going crazy.

- You may be obsessed with the death and preoccupied with the deceased.

- You may find yourself acting socially in ways that are different from before.

- You may find yourself having a number of physical reactions.

- Others will have unrealistic expectations about your mourning and may respond inappropriately to you.

Your grief will bring with it—depending upon the combination of the factors just noted—an intense amount of emotion that will surprise you and those around you. Most of us are unprepared for the global response we have to such a loss. Our expectations tend to be unrealistic. More often than not, we won't receive the help and comfort we need from others.[1]

Your Reflections

1. Describe your most difficult experience of grief so far.

2. What helps you the most when you're struggling with grief?

21

FEELINGS OF GRIEF

I'm overwhelmed by feelings. They're terrible—out of control and like a category five hurricane. There is no sense or reason to them." These are common and painful cries expressed by many. People have said grief is the blackest night of confusion because of all the emotions. Your range of feelings is like a smorgasbord. Each day you have a wide variety to choose from. There will also be daily variations that come and go. You may think they're gone for good…but not so. They disappear, reappear, and overlap. Thankfully, over time they will become less frequent and less intense.

Here's an innovative way to look at feelings:

> Think of a painful feeling as being like a bonfire in a field. At first it is hot, unapproachable. Later it may still smolder. Even later, you can walk on the ground without pain, but you know there is an essence of the fire that still remains. Take your own time, but be sure to walk over the ground again. You must do so because whatever you run away from runs you.[1]

And the feelings hit when least expected.

My Journal

The cemetery. It was Sunday morning. I rounded the curve and saw the cemetery on the right. Acres of green lawn with flowers scattered around. I began to weep. Grief slammed into me, and I was out of control. Joyce was buried here. This is where her body is, and I don't want her body to be here. There's a terrible sense of finality. She's gone and won't be back. I know that. But part of me is still resisting this reality. I want her next to me in the car. But it wasn't going to be. My crying continued like ocean waves as I drove to the gravesite and exchanged the fresh roses for the withered bouquet. So many of the other flowers there were artificial. They were vivid in color but still didn't look real. They weren't the same. Flowers that are real and were once alive and vibrant reflect the pattern of life and death. They wither just as we do.

As I walked back to the car, Shadow was looking at me out the back window. Could he sense what was occurring? It was as if his look said, "I know. Alone is not a pleasant experience." I went up to the car sobbing and held on to him. There is such comfort in a touch— whether it's a person or an animal.

I drove away drained. This will be a long day.

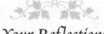

Your Reflections

1. When you visit the resting place of your spouse, what do you experience?

2. Is it a comfort to revisit this place or very painful? Who do you take with you? Who would you like to accompany you?

22

ANGER

W hat are some of the most common feelings and concerns grieving spouses experience? Some of these may describe you and
some may not—at this particular time.

"I feel like I've lost my best friend." And for some, they have. Marriage
holds the greatest potential for intimacy of any relationship. Now the
shared experiences have ceased and the comfort of knowing another
so well, along with an abundance of automatic responses, is gone.

"I am angry." To whom is this directed? Yourself, the doctors, the
hospital, your spouse, to God? Anger is a feeling of displeasure, irri-
tation, and protest. In grief especially, it's a protest, a desire to make
someone pay, to declare the unfairness of the death. We're frustrated,
hurt, afraid, and feeling helpless. Sometimes the anger is expressed
like a missile. It erupts suddenly from the silo. There's no warning. No
alarm sounds. The day has been calm, and suddenly the missile bursts
out. And there is damage. Another day your anger may be expressed
in silent withdrawal. It's subtle, but it's still there. And sometimes the
anger is frozen. It's solid and heavy.

Is anger necessary? Perhaps. I do know it's not wrong. Have you ever
considered the idea that anger is not sin but emotional information?
It's just one of the many expressions of grief. It's here for a purpose.
Because we believe the tragedy or crisis shouldn't have happened, we
look for something or someone to blame—a doctor, a hospital, an organization, a CEO, an accountant, a bus driver, or anyone we perceive

as having somehow participated in the crisis. Sometimes our anger is vented toward anyone who is around, especially family members. You may be angry at everyone around you who hasn't lost anyone because their lives are going on as usual. They have no idea how you feel because they haven't been devastated as you have.

Your Reflections

1. How and when have you experienced anger?

2. What happened?

23

ANGRY AT WHOM?

It may be especially hard to admit you're angry at God. Your anger may be at him for not responding in the way you wanted when your spouse was sick or injured. Or maybe it's because your faith and beliefs didn't seem to work since a healing didn't occur. The distress over the failure of God to respond in the way you needed him can prolong your grief. Tell God your feelings. He can handle it. In fact, anger at God is part of the ancient Jewish tradition. The book of Psalms includes laments that express anger at God for numerous reasons. The anger of grief directed at God is *your response to loss.* It doesn't indicate a lack of faith.

Anger is all right as long as it doesn't get the best of you. And rest assured it will never get the best of God. You may feel like this:

How long, O LORD? Will you forget me forever?
How long will you hide your face from me?
How long must I wrestle with my thoughts
    and every day have sorrow in my heart?
    How long will my enemy triumph over me?
Look on me and answer, O LORD my God,
    Give light to my eyes, or I will sleep in death
    (Psalm 13:1-3).

In time, choose to give up your anger. It has its purpose, yes, but it will outlive it. In spite of all David's angry questions, he came to this place:

But I trust in your unfailing love;
> my heart rejoices in your salvation.
I will sing to the LORD,
> for he has been good to me
> (verses 5-6).

The following are options of how to deal with each part of your anger. By dealing directly with the emotion, you can be free of its controlling power.

- Admit your anger.
- Recognize the cost of keeping your anger.
- Explore God's Word regarding anger.
- Decide if your anger is self-centered or God-centered.
- Recognize that when others hurt God's children, they also hurt God.
- Recognize that God loves you and has your best interest at heart.
- Decide why or at whom you are angry.
- Look at the different parts of your anger.
- Recognize when you're blaming yourself, others, or God. Choose to stop wasting time blaming. Blaming only adds fuel to the anger and is nonproductive.
- Talk about your anger with a friend or counselor.
- Make a conscious decision to become aware of your source of anger and release it to God.

Your Reflections

1. Why not journal about your anger by writing or using a tape recorder?

Here are some statements that may help you get started. Jot down some thoughts to get going.

- I wish I had said...

- I remember when we...

- I wish you had...

- What will happen now that...

- When I think of my anger I think of...

2. Ask a trusted friend to read a portion of your journal and give you some feedback on how he or she thinks you're doing and as a sharing opportunity.

3. Review your journal over a period of two weeks. Do you notice any improvement in the intensity of your anger?

A Closer Look at Anger

Take a moment to break apart your anger. Remember when you were learning to read? You didn't immediately begin reading—you first learned the letters, and then you learned to put them together to get meaning. By breaking apart anger, you can gain a deeper understanding of your hurt.

Your Reflections

1. Determine what you are angry about regarding...

- yourself—

- others—

- God—

- the situation—

Evaluate Your Thoughts

Are you feeling guilty about what you did (or didn't do)? Do these sound familiar?

- "My love wasn't enough."
- "His care could have been better."
- "I should have listened more."
- "If only…"

Is death—especially your own—on your mind? You may realize more than ever before that you will die someday. Your mortality has come to center stage. "If he or she died, I could too." And you could be even more sensitive to the deaths of those you know. "It's difficult now to find any relief from this subject."

You probably tend to focus more on your limitations than your strengths right now. "I feel so much older now." If you're over 40 or 50, it's not just the death of your spouse that creates this feeling but our culture contributes as well. The emphasis upon staying young is everywhere. "Get rid of the gray." "Eliminate wrinkles."

Our bodies grieve as well. "I feel sick most of the time." In grief our immune system is often compromised so we are more susceptible to illnesses, and many of the grief symptoms contribute to this feeling.

Your Reflections

1. What are you feeling right now?

2. Are you experiencing any physical signs of grief? If so, what are they?

25

FEARS

"I live with fear." Loss and fear go hand in hand. We can be afraid of how we'll survive—being alone now and forever, driving, sounds in the night, finances, the reaction of others, and so forth.

You may be a person for whom fear had never found a residence. But now it's moved in. Fear can disable you by crippling your relationships with others and making life more of a chore than it actually is. With fear you imagine the worst, and this leads to anxiety and dread.

> Fear can be debilitating. Some people experience fear in a small number of areas, while others are overwhelmed by it. It is perfectly natural to be fearful. We have experienced the most unexpected tragedy. Common fears include: fearing any situation that remotely resembles how the loved one died, fearing that others we love will be harmed, fearing we will not be able to go on, fearing we will die ourselves, and fearing the simplest activities will lead to tragedy.[1]

Your Reflections

1. Place a check mark by any of the following fears you identify with:

   ___ Fear of a new identity

   ___ Fear of the future

__ Fear of losing control

__ Fear of intimacy (being comforted)

__ Fear of admitting anger at God

__ Fear of facing fear—old memories, anniversary dates, etc.

__ Fear of always feeling the way you do now

__ Fear of not being able to carry on

__ Fear of being overwhelmed

__ Fear of showing emotions

__ Fear of not being "spiritual"

__ Others

Freedom from Fear

Recognizing fears, however big or small, brings about the ability to gain freedom from the constraints of fear. Facing your fears is *a decision to reclaim your life*. It's so easy to get paralyzed between the fear of facing what has happened and the fear of what might be. This is a time to use the strength and wisdom found in the Scriptures. Reading the following verses from the Living Bible aloud several times a day or when fears hit may help you find the stability you're seeking.

> Let him have all your worries and cares, for he is always thinking about you and watching everything that concerns you (1 Peter 5:7).

> He will keep in perfect peace all those who trust in him, whose thoughts turn often to the Lord! (Isaiah 26:3).

> Don't worry about anything; instead, pray about everything; tell God your needs, and don't forget to thank him for his answers. If you do this, you will experience God's peace, which is far more wonderful than the human mind can understand.

His peace will keep your thoughts and your hearts quiet and at rest as you trust in Christ Jesus. And now, brothers, as I close this letter, let me say this one more thing: Fix your thoughts on what is true and good and right. Think about things that are pure and lovely, and dwell on the fine, good things in others. Think about all you can praise God for and be glad about. Keep putting into practice all you learned from me and saw me doing, and the God of peace will be with you (Philippians 4:6-9).

Fear not, for I am with you. Do not be dismayed. I am your God. I will strengthen you; I will help you; I will uphold you with my victorious right hand (Isaiah 41:10).

Your Reflections

1. Describe how you respond to fear when it occurs.

2. Who is aware of your fears? Is that okay?

3. How can you apply the scriptures in this chapter to your situation?

26

Depression and Grief

There is always a temptation to shut down when painful feelings come. This is a normal response when you're grieving, but it often leads to depression.

The deeper your depression, the more paralyzing your sense of helplessness becomes. You feel passive and resigned. Everything seems out of focus. You're in a deep, dark pit, cold and isolated. There doesn't seem to be a way out. Depression can blind you to the positive realities of life. It narrows your perception of the world. You feel all alone, as though no one else cares about you.

When depression seeps in, you brood about the past, become overly introspective, and are preoccupied with recurring negative thoughts. And worse yet, your mind replays the same negative images over and over again. And to add to the pain of your grief, you're oversensitive to what others say and do. And when others don't know how to respond to your grief properly, your pain can be intensified as you feel even more misunderstood.

Depression affects you spiritually and can change the way you see God. It's hard to believe in a loving and personal God who knows the answers and wants you to succeed when he seems so far off. These feelings aren't new. The psalmist reflected on them as well:

> Have mercy on me, O LORD, for I am weak;
> O LORD, heal me, for my bones are troubled.
> My soul also is greatly troubled;
> But You, O LORD—how long?

Return, O Lord, deliver me!
Oh, save me for Your mercies' sake!
For in death there is no remembrance of You;
In the grave who will give You thanks?

I am weary with my groaning;
All night I make my bed swim;
I drench my couch with my tears.
My eye wastes away because of grief;
It grows old because of all my enemies
(Psalm 6:2-7 nkjv).

Instead of experiencing peace, joy, and the light of God in your life, you feel just the opposite. You feel empty. Often Christians who are depressed feel even worse because of their false belief that it is a sin for a Christian to be depressed. *This is not true!* And most depressions are not brought on by sin.

Your Reflections

These three questions have been very helpful for people when evaluating how they're feeling.

1. What is it like when you feel depressed?

___ a slate-gray afternoon

___ a cold, drizzling rain

___ a hot, oppressively humid day

___ a freezing morning with a bitter wind

___ a dull, overcast sky

___ a season of ankle-deep mud and slush

2. Right now, what type of weather forecast best describes where you are in the process of dealing with your loss?

    __ stormy conditions

    __ partly cloudy

    __ heavy rain

    __ a thaw

    __ chilly days

    __ sunny days ahead

    __ gentle spring breezes blowing

3. Where on the scale would you place your current grief process?

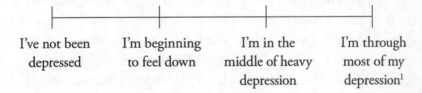

I've not been depressed	I'm beginning to feel down	I'm in the middle of heavy depression	I'm through most of my depression[1]

Avoiding Pain

In grief, the presence of pain can seem constant. We try to avoid its presence with little success, or so it's been in my journey.

A Cavern of Memories

Our minds are such mysteries. The thinking process is who we are, and it encompasses our present life and the storehouse of memories (good and bad). The mind can resemble a cavern with a labyrinth of crevices and vast rooms of darkness. Within many of these are memories made up of bits and pieces from the long-ago past as well as the most recent past. And they're not always factual, but more like a collage that includes feelings (light and intense), images, and fragments that our minds spread out on a table to create stories.

Sometimes we forget what we would like to remember and remember what we would like to forget. Pain can be so intense we wish it could be banished. But we know it's still there. Perhaps in taking it out, holding it, and looking at it, the pain will diminish. At least that's what I tell others about their traumatic memories. And for them it usually happens that way. But in grief, some memories are too fresh, too real, too close, and too soon to examine.

My Journal

My cavern of memories. Every now and then, like this morning, I venture into the cavern of memories of the last ten days of Joyce's life.

I visit images of her in a situation where I can't help, don't understand what she's trying to convey, and feel her apparent pain so much that I feel totally helpless. That now translates into the agony of not having answered her distress...as well as knowing there aren't any human answers. Visiting this image just generates pain. Will it ever leave? Hopefully, but for now it continues to live in the cavern, knowing that I know about it and will call it up again...even though I know its impact. This morning I entered, knowing the risk. I did so perhaps hoping the pain would have faded in its intensity. If there is the possibility of asking questions in heaven, perhaps I could just wait for that time...but I don't. I don't know why I continue to revisit that cavern. It could be that I prefer not to have an answer to discuss because it could magnify my pain.

> Grieving is more like a maze of emotions than an elevator that starts at the bottom and arrives at the penthouse of peace and understanding. Like a maze, we go forward a bit and then back over the same territory. If we learn to love and accept ourselves even as we are emotionally weaving through the maze, we may begin to see our humanness and our brokenness as a threshold to personal growth. In any case, it is important to assure yourself, no matter how "crazy" and lost in the maze you may feel, that you do come out on the other side and that you are not alone.[1]

God is obviously aware of our need for encouragement each morning. The Scripture is full of people who have known grief, who have faced mornings of pain and sorrow. David spoke eloquently of his dread of the morning when he wrote in Psalm 73:14, "All day long I have been plagued; I have been punished every morning." When we are hurting, mornings can seem like punishment.

While waiting upon the Lord for deliverance from his troubles, Jeremiah cries out to God, "This I call to mind and therefore I have hope: Because of the LORD's great love we are not consumed, for his compassions never fail. They are new every morning; great is your faithfulness" (Lamentations 3:21-23). Jeremiah was still in the midst of trouble when he said those words, but he chose to dwell on what would bring him hope for a better day...maybe not tomorrow or the next day, but in God's timing.

David said this about the morning: "Weeping may remain for a night, but rejoicing comes in the morning" (Psalm 30:5). In Psalm 59:16 he wrote, "I will sing of your strength, in the morning I will sing of your love; for you are my fortress, my refuge in times of trouble."[2]

Your Reflections

1. What memories are very special to you?

2. What memories would you like to forget?

28

I Believe

You feel like Humpty Dumpty. You've fallen off the wall and you know all the king's horses and all the king's men are never going to be able to put you together again.

Joyce Landorf, *Mourning Song*

In the weeks and months following the death of someone we love, we often feel like Humpty Dumpty. That's the only way to describe it. We feel broken. We hurt so much that our pain seems tangible. We move cautiously and uncertainly because our nerve endings are all on alert, sensitive to the slightest stimulus. We breathe shallowly, afraid to take a deep breath for fear our lungs will press too harshly on our aching hearts. There are times when the atmosphere around us is charged with our anguish and dread. We long for the days when life was simpler and sweeter.

There is a great difference between *our King* and Humpty Dumpty's! Our King can put Humpty Dumpty back together again. In fact, our King sent his Son, Jesus, to be broken for us so that he could put us back together better than we were before. This doesn't mean our pain isn't real. It *is* very real, just as Christ's pain was real when he wept for Lazarus and hung on the cross. What it does mean is that we can have hope in the midst of our pain. We can turn to our loving heavenly Father, knowing he will see us through this pain and knowing that Christ understands because he has felt pain himself.

We have an Advocate and a Helper who will assist us—if we ask—as

97

we grapple with the reality of death, as we struggle to find acceptance—even joy—in the face of our very personal suffering. If we
are faithful to the task at hand, if we determine to walk through this
storm, continually calling upon our Father Advocate Helper, we will
arrive at the other side with a renewed understanding of our lives—
and of life in general. We will learn to live more joyously because we
have faced death.

For today, face with courage and determination the daunting task
of examining the broken pieces of your life. Give full attention to the
pieces of your sorrow, your anger, your fear, your disillusionment, your
faltering faith. Do this because your job in this rebuilding process is
to hand each piece to your heavenly Father as he asks for them. Then
watch in awe as he puts them back together in a new and better pattern of living.[1]

Each day your feelings will vary. Some days will be better than
others. Everyday activities that used to be commonplace may take on
new meanings.

My Journal

Roses. I stopped to buy roses at Von's, as I often did. Joyce loved a
mixed-color bouquet—pastels, variegated blossoms, rich red or white
roses. As I stood looking at the flowers, I could feel the waves of emotion beginning. As I walked up to the multitude of bunched flowers,
they seemed to rise and ambush my emotions. The sorrow, which is
in a floating state inside me, rushed to the surface. This was so much
harder than I thought. I wanted a bouquet to take home as I always
did, but I also planned to take one for Joyce's grave. I vacillated between
control and falling apart. When I reached the checkstand the woman
commented on their beauty and freshness and all was okay until she
asked, "Are these for your wife?" I fought to keep myself together
while wondering what to do or say to her so she wouldn't feel bad
about asking.

I said, "One bouquet is for home and the other is for her gravesite. It's been three weeks." Her response was very gracious. As I left I could feel my reserve crumbling. I kept the flowers in front of my face and walked quickly through the store. By the time I was in the parking lot, silent sobs came. I was hoping I wouldn't run into anyone I knew. I felt overwhelmed and sobbed driving home. My mind and professional training as a counselor told me how normal this was, but the ache of loss was so much. *Will it be like this each time?* I wondered. *Or is it because I was facing a longtime routine without Joyce?* It's the "without" that is the hardest.

In times of loss and sorrow, we, as people of faith, have to "believe against the grain." In our weakness God reveals his strength, and with him we can do more than we thought possible. Faith means clinging to God in spite of our circumstances. It means following him when we can't see him. It means being faithful to him when we don't feel like it. Resilient people have a creed that says "I believe!" and they affirm their creed daily. In essence they say:

- I believe God's promises are true.
- I believe heaven is real.
- I believe God will see me through.
- I believe nothing can separate me from God's love.
- I believe God has work for me to do.

"Believing against the grain" means having a survivalist attitude. Not only can we survive, but out of this pain and suffering we can create something good.[2] We need to cry out, "God, help me believe!"

Your Reflections

1. How do you wish God would put you together again?

2. What is the most difficult for you to believe about God at this time?

RELEARNING YOUR LIFE

Do you know what it's like to be stuck in a traffic jam? Minutes drag like hours. Your car creeps at a snail's pace. Other drivers vent their frustration by trying to sneak past on the shoulder. Truckers linger, creating huge gaps in the traffic. If only you could get around them! If only you could get to the other side of the mess.

And then you finally do. You move past the roadblock and hurl down the highway free of obstructions, rapidly leaving your frustration behind. You're free! You've gotten to the other side.

Grieving has another side too.[1]

"How will I know when I've reached the other side? What will be the indication that the worse of the pain is over? How will I feel when I've recovered from my loss?" Have you asked these questions? We want to know when and how! Recovery is essential for any kind of loss, but the actual recovery period will vary depending on the type of loss and its intensity.

Have you been in the hospital for an operation? If so, you know the process. After the operation is over, you're taken to a recovery room, where you stay for a few hours until the effects of the anesthetic wears off. The term "recovery" is a bit misleading for this room. It certainly doesn't mean total recovery. It means making sure you've adjusted to the effects of the operation so you're ready for the healing and the healthier you. And it's the same with grief. "Recovery" doesn't mean getting back to the way you were before. That won't happen. You have to develop a new life, a new normal. "Recovery" is really relearning your life.

During the early months of grief, relearning is like having to get off the main highway every so many miles because the direct route is under construction. The road signs route you through little towns you hadn't expected to visit and over bumpy roads you weren't planning on bouncing around on. You're basically traveling in the appropriate direction. On the map, however, the course you're following has the look of shark's teeth instead of a straight line. Although you are gradually getting where you want to be, you sometimes doubt you'll ever meet up with the finished highway.[2] Haven't you felt this way? I have…and my friends have.

Hopefully friends and relatives will be a source of support in your recovery. But their response will probably be mixed. You will hear supportive words that comfort as well as statements that wound. One phrase that gives no comfort, "I'm sorry," will become repetitive and painful. Some people won't know how to respond to you and will soon disappear. Some will be invasive and intrusive and tell you what do to, what to feel, and how long it will take to heal. It's all right to be selective in who you want around and who you don't. You need those who will be there as long as it takes. But after a while you may feel forgotten.

> In the immediate days following a loss, we are often bombarded with visitors, food, offers to help, phone calls, flowers and condolences. Then we see the ten-day syndrome in action, most major news stories get about ten days of coverage in the media and then it's old news—on with the new. The grief experience is often similar. As the days roll by, the calls, condolences and comfort lessen. It may appear as if all are trying to get back to "their" world before the tragedy happened. Meanwhile, we are just beginning the long and difficult road of grief—needing more support than ever.[3]

More than anything you want someone who can be fully present with you. And when you have it, count it as a gift.

My Journal

Presence. The hole in my life was still there, but I didn't feel it quite so much because a friend was with me. And that's what happens when friends come to be with me at this time—they're a covering for the pain and sorrow. Nothing can really fill the hole in me at this time, but for a while its presence is dulled because of the presence of a friend. The feeling of "without" is dulled by the support of those who care. Presence is what our lives are about. It was the presence of Joyce that helped make my life meaningful. It's the presence of others that make life livable. And God's presence fills in the gap of unanswered questions about life and suffering. When answers don't come God's presence is the comforter. When others aren't here, his presence is sufficient if I will just remember he is here. His words, "I will never leave you," are true!

The other morning I felt <u>presence</u>, and it happened at a time and in a place where I didn't expect it. I sat in my doctor's office, giving information to the nurse. This was my family doctor who's experienced cancer in his own life. He was present at Joyce's memorial service. But I never expected that seeing him would be such a trigger to my emotions. When the door opened and he walked in, I looked at his face and began to cry. He didn't say a word. He sat down in front of me and was silent. Behind his beard I sensed his own struggle with his thoughts and feelings. I could see his pain and the compassion in his eyes. And so with a waiting room filled with a dozen people and a staff of 15 to oversee, he sat with me in a relaxed and unhurried manner for the next 15 minutes. We talked. He asked a number of insightful questions. We cried and we laughed, but more than anything else it was his presence with me that meant so much. When I left I thanked God for this experience. My feelings were just hovering beneath the surface all morning but that was acceptable. After all, what choice do we have than to accept them because we can't really control them. And they are here for a purpose. They provide "vocabulary for our suffering," in the words of singer/songwriter Michael Card.

It dawned on me that I had experienced a "ministry of presence" that morning, which was a gift. I often teach this concept to chaplains and counselors, and now once again I experienced it firsthand. My doctor had "shown up" as though he had to come in to see me. He didn't really "do," but he was with me and being who he was. He listened more than he talked. He sat in silence with me. And he gave me a calm, accepting presence. Above all, he walked through my pain with me and I felt his caring. This man was a compassionate companion when I needed it most.

Your Reflections

1. In what ways are you relearning your world?

2. Who are the people who have been here for you? How have they been helpful?

NOT QUITE MYSELF

R ecovery" or "relearning" does not mean a once-and-for-all con-clusion to your loss and grief. It is a twofold process involving regaining our ability to function as we once did and resolving and making sense of our loss in our lives. But, yes, there is something else to recovery.

In a sense, you will never recover completely because you will never be exactly the way you were before. Loss changes you. As someone once asked in a counseling session, "If I can't be the way I was before and I never recover completely, what is all this about recovery? I'm confused. What does it mean? How can you recover and not recover fully?"

I can offer a simple but good example. I still have a scar from an incision made during an operation when I was a child. In a sense, it serves as a reminder that I had that experience. Recovery is like a scar from an operation, but it is in such a sensitive place that on occasion you will feel it ache again. And you can't predict when it will happen. I will continue to use the word "recovery" because we're so familiar with it, but with a new, augmented meaning.

Recovery is feeling better. Recovery means claiming your circum-stances, instead of letting your circumstances claim your happiness. Recovery is finding new meaning for living without the fear of future abandonment. Recovery is being able to enjoy fond memories with-out having them precipitate painful feelings of loss, guilt, regret, or remorse. Recovery is acknowledging that it is perfectly all right to feel bad from time to time and to talk about those feelings no matter how those around you react. Recovery is being able to forgive others when they say or do things that you know are based on their lack of knowledge about grief. Recovery is one day realizing that your ability to talk about the loss you've experienced is in fact helping another person get through his or her grief.[1]

Recovery means reinvesting in life by looking for new relationships and new dreams. A newfound source of joy is possible. You may feel odd though. You could very well feel uncomfortable with whatever is new. You may feel that to experience joy again is somehow wrong. And there's the fear that if you begin to hope or trust again, you could experience another loss.

Remember the *source* of joy. It is the Lord. The psalmist states that God "clothes us with joy" (Psalm 30:11). He is the One who extends to you the invitation to reinvest in life.

Moving On

I will exalt you, O LORD,
　　for you lifted me out of the depths
　　and did not let my enemies gloat over me.
O LORD my God, I called to you for help
　　and you healed me.
O LORD, you brought me up from the grave;
　　you spared me from going down into the pit.

Sing to the LORD, you saints of his;
　　praise his holy name.
For his anger lasts only a moment,
　　but his favor lasts a lifetime;
　　weeping may remain for a night,
　　but rejoicing comes in the morning.

When I felt secure, I said,
　　"I will never be shaken."
O LORD, when you favored me,
　　you made my mountain stand firm;
but when you hid your face,
　　I was dismayed.

To you, O Lord, I called;
  to the Lord I cried for mercy:
"What gain is there in my destruction,
  in my going down into the pit?
Will the dust praise you?
  Will it proclaim your faithfulness?
Hear, O Lord, and be merciful to me;
  O Lord, be my help."

You turned my wailing into dancing;
  you removed my sackcloth and clothed me with joy,
  that my heart may sing to you and not be silent.
O Lord my God, I will give you thanks forever
(Psalm 30).

Did you notice what was said in this psalm about grief and moving on? In grief we sometimes feel as if we're going to die. Have you felt that way?

In grief we also have times when we feel God is hiding his face from us. Have you felt that way? I have.

My Journal

Not quite myself. I know that I'm not quite myself. I'm not an avoider, but I find that my limit of being with others has diminished. It used to be there were no limits whereas now they exist.

I know that I'm not quite myself because I listen to my voice when I talk with others. There's a change in my response. I don't know if others hear it. If they listen carefully and compare me to several months ago, my tone has changed. My volume and enunciation are different. If I'm aware of it, others have got to be aware as well. My interest level has waned. The excitement for some activities and events has waned. In Psalm 13 (NASB) it says,

How long, O Lord? Will You forget me forever?
How long will You hide Your face from me?

How long shall I take counsel in my soul,
    having sorrow in my heart all the day…
Consider and answer me, O LORD my God;
Enlighten my eyes, or I will sleep the sleep of death.

That last phrase can mean "put the light back in my eyes." Grief can change the way we look or even cover our faces with masks. It can take the sparkle from our eyes and create faces of sadness. It can take the lilts and expressions out of our voices. But God can and will bring the interest back into our lives as we look to him to change our responses.

Your Reflections

1. In what ways are you different now?

2. In what ways are you reinvesting in life?

3. What will help you reinvest in life even more?[2]

4. Describe how you are recovering.

THE CHOICE OF RECOVERY

In this journey of grief we eventually discover that our weeping will not last forever. Are there clothes of mourning you would like to exchange for clothes of joy? Do you realize you have a choice in your recovery? Most people don't have a choice in their loss, but *everyone has a choice in his or her recovery.* The change in your identity, relationships, new roles, and even abilities can be either positive or negative. *This* is where you have choices.

I've seen people choose to live in denial and move ahead as though nothing really happened. I've seen those stuck in the early stages of grief as they choose to live in bitterness and blame. Some people become so hardened and angry that it is difficult to be around them for extended periods of time. They have made a choice. Their views and responses are *not* the fault of other people or of God. Since life is full of losses, we have the option of doing something constructive or destructive with our sorrows.

The journey of grief involves relearning your world—a world changed drastically by the death of your spouse. What you experience now will never be experienced the way it was before. The life patterns and daily routines you once had exist no longer. You can't do what you used to do in the same way or get back everything you had at one time. Changes have been forced upon you. Like it or not, you've been put back in school so you can relearn what was once familiar and automatic but now has new nuances or is completely changed.

What will you need to relearn? Your physical surroundings. The rooms and furniture are reminders of your mate, as is your residence.

There will be good memories that are comforting as well as painful ones you wish you could avoid. What do you leave out, and what do you put away and when? What do you keep, and what do you dispose of? What about clothing worn on special occasions, colognes, perfumes, the bed that was shared, the car, furniture your spouse loved and you hated, gifts you gave, and gifts you received? All these entail decisions that need to be faced...but not immediately.

Your personal relationships need to be relearned for they too will experience upheavals. You are different, and so are most people you know. Others will also be grieving in their own ways. Some will be supportive of your grief and walk with you in it, while others will be impatient with you and want you to move faster than you're comfortable with. Some will want to talk about the situation, while others will avoid the subject. Friends—especially couple friends—may vanish over time because you are no longer part of the couple world. You may feel responsible to help the grieving of others, including your children, grandchildren, your spouse's parents, your spouse's siblings, but you hardly have energy enough for yourself. If your spouse was more involved in the lives of your children, where does this leave you? What will you do now? Can you take over all the roles and responsibilities your spouse filled?

You'll also need to relearn who *you* are. Your identity and place in the world has changed. You have to adapt your daily routine and activities. Your hopes, dreams, desires, and expectations have experienced a forced upheaval. Who are you now that you are alone? And what do you call yourself? Single? Widow? Widower? The first time you see the new label by your name or write it you may be shocked. I was. I bought a house for my daughter, and when I received the paperwork and title for the home I noticed right next to my name was the word "widower." My reaction? "Why did they have to put that there?" Yes, the word was true, but it was also uncomfortable to me.

Your Reflections

1. Describe what you will no longer be able to do.

2. In what ways are your personal relationships different?

3. How will you describe yourself to friends? To strangers?

A Look at Me

You will probably also be relearning your spiritual life in some ways. Questions that were never asked before may come to the surface. New answers may be discovered, but there may be a number of unanswered ones as well.

Many people experience a crisis of faith when a loved one dies. Others find their faith deepened by their reliance upon the Lord. You may have relied on your spouse for spiritual leadership and guidance, so now you feel cut adrift. You may have prayed together, and now you miss that as well. And you may be like Job who, after all he went through (losing all he had), ended up with a new relationship. Many talk about all Job received again later in life—children, possessions, and wealth. But what he really got back was God, as evidenced in this verse: "My ears had heard of you but now my eyes have seen you" (Job 42:5).[1]

Is there any kind of criteria a person can use in the process of grieving to evaluate whether or not recovery is occurring? Yes. At the end of this book, just before the Notes, is a "Grief Recovery Evaluation" exercise. As you go through it, the conclusions you reach may help you decide where you are in your recovery. On a scale of 0 to 10 (0 meaning "not at all" and 10 meaning "total recovery in that area"), rate yourself in response to each question. This evaluation is geared toward the loss of a spouse.[2] I encourage you to fill out the chart, but if you don't feel ready, wait. You'll know when it's time. Once you do it, repeat it every three months to note your progress. You also might consider asking an objective friend to help you.

THE GIFT OF WRITING

Grief recovery is a back-and-forth process. One of the better ways to identify your progress is through a personal journal. This will provide proof that you are making progress even when your feelings say otherwise. Your journal is your *private* property and *is not* for anyone else to read. It's an expression of what *you* are feeling right now in your recovery. It can be written in any style, but it's best done longhand so your thoughts flow and you can add art, drawings, illustrations as you feel like it. You can also put in simple statements, poems, and prayers that reflect your journey.

If you'd like help getting started, here are some questions you can ask and answer.

- What do I miss most about my spouse?
- What do I wish I had asked or said to my spouse?
- What do I wish I had done or not done?
- What do I wish my spouse had said or not said?
- What do I wish my spouse had done or not done?
- What did I value most about our relationship?
- What was hurtful or angering about our relationship?
- What special moments do I remember about my spouse? What memories will I keep alive?
- What will I keep with me to cherish as a part of my spouse and our relationship?
- What living situation is difficult to deal with without my spouse?[1]

Journaling is taking what is in your heart and mind and transferring it elsewhere. Your expressions may be a mixture of pain, sadness, and hope. Mine has encompassed all that and more. This is part of the ongoing process of saying goodbye.

- You may find it helpful to make time every day to write at least a short paragraph in your journal. At the end of the week, review what you've written to note any steps (small or large) of progress toward recovery. Writing at least a line or two every day is the most effective way to keep a journal.

- Some people write in their journals a few times each week, reviewing them at the end of the week and at the end of each month.

The following steps and information were used by Dave in his recovery. He's allowed me to share them in the hope they'll help you too.

How to Journal
- Date every entry.
- Start writing, drawing, or doodling.
- Be honest.
- Be open.
- Be willing to risk—remember, it's private.

In addition, you can use some or all of the following 20 journaling styles.

1. *Captured moments:* Write about an event or place that triggers memories or feelings for you. For examples, revisit a special place, recall something your loved one did or you did together, remember conversations shared with others.

2. *Stepping-stones:* Write about times in your relationship. For example, what you did, where you met, where you vacationed, places you went on dates, holidays you celebrated.

3. *Topic of the day:* Number the days of the month on a page. Beside each number write a subject topic that you can think about and write about: 1/1—job, 1/2—money, 1/3—house, 1/4—parent, 1/5—child.

4. *Character sketch:* Try to see yourself as others see you. For example, journal on a particular scripture, such as Matthew 7:3-5. What are the planks in your eye? What do people (or a particular person) do that angers you or makes you crazy?

5. *Current milestones:* Write about current events. For example, moving, selling the house, making new friends.

6. *Write letters to God, lost loved ones, yourself, or others:* A good time to write letters is when there is unfinished business with the person who is gone or when there is a desire to experience closure of unresolved issues. *The key is not to send them.* This makes the letter a safe, nonthreatening atmosphere. For example, write letters that express your deep emotions (anger, grief, hostility, resentment, opinions, affections).

7. *List opposites:* Make a list of emotion and event words. Then under each one write down what comes to mind when you think of the word. For example under "Glad" you might write: "Positive: last Christmas, Leroy, Shadow. Negative: Will I ever feel glad again?"

8. *KISS (keep it short and simple):* Write down brief sentences about what you're feeling or experiencing. For example: "I'm scared and feel like I'm going to break."

9. *Theme word for the week:* Choose a word or topic and write about it every day. For example, loneliness, confusion, change.

10. *Quick starts:* Begin with a question or statement and write about any thoughts or feelings it triggers. Keep a list of possible questions or statements on a page in your journal. For example, "I'm excited about…" "I'm alone and it's…" "My secret is…" "I wish…" "I'm afraid of…" "I always…" "I never…"

11. *Trigger memories:* Use photographs, videos, recordings, and other objects to trigger thoughts, feelings, and memories. Write about them freely.

12. *Visit a favorite place:* Go to a place where you can relax and feel comfortable. Let the thoughts and feelings flow. Write about them as they come. Don't worry about grammar, spelling, or composition.

13. *Clustering:* Use both sides of your brain. Choose a keyword or phrase to trigger your thoughts, feelings, and memories. Group them together under topic. Write about each cluster. Keep it simple. It's okay to repeat yourself. Try to complete your thoughts in one sitting. Here's a "love cluster" sample:

Lost   Hope
  Empty   Peace
     Fear   Salvation
       Loss   Jesus
                                                    God
                          Love
        Marriage   Sunshine
        Children   Blue Skies
    Grandchildren   Flowers
Valuable   Hope

14. *Secondary losses:* Write about other related losses you've experienced. For example, someone to go fishing with.

15. *Peripheral events:* Write about events that led up to or surrounded the loss. For example, illness, a fight, poor communication.

16. *Create a card:* Create a card for a special occasion such as a birthday, anniversary, Mother's Day, or Father's Day. For example, make a birthday card and include everything you can think of that helped your loved one make his or her birthday special. Include your memories of special celebrations.

17. *Journaling:* Write about how you feel about writing or how you feel about what you've been writing.

18. *Time line:* Begin with a date or range of dates. For example, do a chronological blessing time line. Start with the earliest blessing you remember receiving. The same format can be used for other topics too. For example, try combining a loss and blessing time line. Start with your losses, then add the blessings.

19. *List of 100:* Using a topic or sentence starter, list as many responses as possible. For examples, "Things I like about…" "Things I don't like about…" "Things that have changed…" "Things that I fear…" "Things that are blessings…" "Things I remember about…"

20. *Egg symbol:* Draw a simple picture to represent your feelings about your loss. Redraw it periodically, making changes that reflect where you are currently. For example, draw an egg. At the beginning of your loss, it might be in a thousand pieces like Humpty Dumpty after he fell. As time passes, sometimes it will look put back together…and sometimes it will have pieces missing.[2]

All of these suggestions can be part of the process of helping you take the important steps of saying goodbye to your mate and beginning to create and adapt to your new life.

Your journal is yours to say and feel what is in your heart and mind. It is your way of crystallizing the feelings of loss. Dealing with your feelings one at a time in a written, tangible form is a good way to "own" those feelings and respond to them in an organized way. Grief is a tangle of feelings, and writing them down is a great way to isolate and adjust to each one.

Monitor what you write. When you see yourself writing more about what is happening *today* and less about the one you've lost, you'll know that healing and adjustment are indeed taking place, though it may seem painfully slow. Look for signs of progress.

Remember: It is *your* journal! Use it for *your* benefit.[3]

34

EXPRESSIONS OF GRIEF

Don't be afraid to recognize how you're feeling. Here are some expressions of my grief taken from my journal.

My Journal

A quiet life. Joyce was one of those rare individuals who made a difference. At the gravesite service our pastor said, "You will find a person's birth date and the date they died on their headstone or marker separated by a dash. It's not either of those dates that are important, but the dash represents what the person did or who they were between those dates." That small seemingly insignificant dash is what our life together was all about. Joyce's life and lifestyle stood out—not in a blaring, attention-seeking way, but in her own quiet, unpretentious manner.

Some people teach and minister by what they say or what they put down on paper. Joyce didn't write it in a book. She wrote it with her life. She didn't stand in front of hundreds of people teaching and instructing them. No, she taught it with her presence, her consistent presence with the Lord, and sharing with one person at a time. It was the way she answered the phone and put the caller at ease with her voice and words. She didn't see herself as a trained counselor, and what she knew and shared could never be acquired in a school. Joyce's ability and gifts came from another source—an ongoing relationship with her Lord and his Word.

She was so consistent with how she treated everyone, no matter who they were. Her life was fulfillment of Colossians 3:13-16, for she was gracious, kind, humble, gentle, and patient, whether she was with someone in person or talking on the phone. She cared—and it showed. She was concerned—and it showed. She wanted to help—and it showed. She wanted to meet other people's needs first, even at the end when it came to whether to have another surgery to prolong her life. She wanted what Sheryl and I wanted more than what she wanted. We had to tell her not to decide based on us and our desires but on her desire and what she felt God was directing her to do. We had to relinquish what we wanted, and in doing so we were actually saying goodbye.

My Journal

How long? When you're a child and you're riding in a car with your parents, it doesn't take long for you to ask, "When are we going to get there? How far is it? How long?" And it's not that we ask it once, but we do so repeatedly regardless of the answer. We want to know how many hours and minutes we're going to be stuck in the car, as though arriving at the destination is the solution to our confinement and discomfort. We want the freedom that arrival brings us. As a child we hope to hear, "Not long. We're almost there."

In our lifetimes there will be significant events tattooed on our brains so the images—the sights and sounds—are always with us. They may be events in which we're the leading actors or just part of the supporting cast. We may be participants or just spectators, but in either case we're drawn into the drama in a unique manner. I remember where I was and what I was doing when I heard about the assassination of President Kennedy, when the first shuttle exploded, when the Gulf War broke out, and when the twin towers in New York were hit.

I remember the phone conversation with Loma Linda Hospital on March 15, 1990, when my son, Matthew, was in ICU and the words,

"You need to be here as soon as possible" came over the line. And I will always remember saying the words, "How long?"

And later Joyce said them too. "How long do I have if I don't have the surgery?" Joyce asked as she looked at her oncologist. For she too was a traveler—not in a car, but in the journey of life here on earth. The words carried an immense form of finality, as if one door would be closing forever and a new one opening.

"How long do I have here with my family?" was being asked.

And at the end of her journey there would be a release...from the pain, the discomfort, the confusion, the struggle.

We who will be left behind take on new forms of pain and discomfort and confusion and struggle with her absence.

This time Joyce was on a journey whose destination really was the solution to her confinement and discomfort. She was trading what she had on earth for a new life and eventually a new body. This is what awaits us. She just arrived there sooner than us.

"How long?" The answer came, but it didn't come from me. I was stunned into silence.

Her answer came, but it wasn't the estimate guess her doctor gave. It came from someone else in an inaudible voice. Did Joyce hear it? I think she knew. Her journey was almost over when she asked "How long?"

"Not long at all, Joyce. Soon...very soon."

So goodbye for now.

My Journal

'Til death do you part. It was only a Hallmark movie. It was pleasant and nostalgic. The young couple married at the conclusion of the movie, and the minister pronounced the words, "'til death do you part." We said those five words at our marriage ceremony. They were part of the tradition. We expected to say them and gave little thought to their meaning. But like many other words, we soon forget them. Perhaps

we are unable to understand their significance when we're young and assume our lives go on forever. Yes, there's meaning to them, but probably for other couples. But then one day you're alone. Your life partner is gone and the words, "'til death do you part" have become reality. It's like a self-fulfilling prophecy. It's come true. It's one thing to say the words, to know they're part of the commitment, to perhaps remember them occasionally, but it's another to experience their reality.

It's so final. It leaves you alone. You have a sense of isolation. It's a feeling of separation. The only balance to this is the knowledge that this is just a temporary separation. It's not final. Perhaps that needs to be part of the ceremony. "'Til death do you part on earth. But as believers in Christ, you'll meet again in heaven." That is our hope based on God's promises.

Your Reflections

1. How did your spouse impact the lives of others?

2. What scriptures did your spouse most reflect in his or her life?

35

WHEN YOU SEEM STUCK

Grief travels at its own pace—slow...slower...and at a crawl. It's uncontrollable. You wonder when will it lift or when will it get better. You struggle with your feelings and your thoughts.

My Journal

"The Best and Worst of Times." There is a phrase that is often used. It's been running through my head at various times. And when it does I wonder... I wonder if this is beginning to describe where I am on certain occasions. I'm not sure of this either, but I connect with it in some way. The phrase is "It was the best of times and the worst of times." It comes from *A Tale of Two Cities* by Charles Dickens. I can say with all certainty that what I've been going through has been the worst of times, but I know eventually there will be a shift. Even now there have been some positive times and blessings. I've grown emotionally and spiritually, discovered how deeply others are concerned, and been encouraged by those who have continuously been supportive. Would I say this is actually some of the best of times? Perhaps, but that might be stretching it because it's only the three-month mark of Joyce's homegoing. Perhaps my mind can say at times it's the best, but my heart is lagging behind. When they will change places I can't tell, but I know someday they will.

My Journal

Joyce's book. Once again this week has been the best of times and the worst of times. The way others reach out with cards and calls and invitations and getting together is so helpful and I am so grateful.

But several factors have led to disruptive, out-of-control experiences. Coming back from an intense ministry trip to Colorado where I needed to put my own grief on hold was a contributor, as was the Christmas season with all its festivities and memories. I've shared so much with others about the three-month anniversary date being a time when grief intensifies, so perhaps this too has added to the off-balance feel of the past few days. A major factor was completing a project for Sheryl that Joyce began in 2001 and only completed the first half. This "Mother's Book of Memories" about her own mother, her own life, and her thoughts about her daughter turned out to be much more difficult emotionally than I ever imagined. It brought back so much and accentuated the sense of a missing person in my life. Yet it was good to do this in many ways, such as taking the opportunity to review and put memories in writing so they won't be forgotten, discovering some new stories about Joyce that I didn't know, and having the opportunity to be creative in putting this project together. This is Joyce's Christmas gift to Sheryl this year, which will be such a surprise.

Then Joyce's remaining aunt called one evening. Joyce loved her dearly. It was good to hear from her but also sad because it was a reminder of the frailty of life and the deterioration of our natural bodies. I heard her pleasant voice say during our conversation about her moving to an assisted living home, "Norm, I'm not really Kay anymore. I'm not on the road to Zanzibar. I'm on the road to Alzheimer's."

One more trigger and eventually one more hole in my life.

Your Reflections

1. What has been the worst time for you up to this point?

2. What has been the best time?

Unresolved Grief

There are occasions when your forward progress may be disrupted. Counselors often describe this as "unresolved grief." There are many reasons for this, and some of them may overlap. If this has happened to you, sometimes it's a matter of wanting to hold on to your spouse.

One result is when grief is *absent*. Absent grief is just what it sounds like. As strange as it sounds, there are no feelings of grief or mourning. It's as though the loss never occurred. There is a significant amount of denial in this response. Or you may exhibit minimal signs of grief. People around you wonder what is wrong or reinforce your false composure.[1]

A *minimizer* is a spouse who is aware of feelings of grief but works to lessen the feelings, diluting them through a variety of rationalizations, often using spiritual clichés. One example is when a person talks about how he or she is back to normal routines very quickly. On a conscious level, you may seem to be working and conforming to society's message to quickly "get over" grief and move on. But internally the blocked feelings of grief continue to build and fester. With no outlet, emotional strain and tension result.

You may believe grief is something to be quickly *thought* through but not *felt*. This is typically an intellectual process in which words become a substitute for the expression of true feelings. You may believe feelings of grief are threatening because they involve pain.

We all have our own ways to express grief. Some individuals are *intuitive grievers.* For them feelings are intensely experienced. If this is where you are, you want to cry…and you need to cry.

Others are *instrumental grievers.* More men than women fall into this category. You *think* of your grief more than actually feeling it. The feelings you do have are less intense. You tend not to cry or seek help, and you have a general reluctance to talk about feelings. You need to control yourself and your environment, so you use a problem-solving approach to accomplish this.

Still others are *blended grievers.* They have elements of both intuitive and instrumental grievers, but with a greater emphasis on one or the other.[2]

There are people who won't let any painful feelings emerge. There is a blockage, and in some cases it could be from childhood trauma.

Inhibited grief involves the repression of some of the normal grief responses. Other symptoms, such as bodily complaints, may take their place. Stomachaches, loss of energy, and headaches are some of the more common responses. You may be able to grieve over only certain aspects of what was lost. Perhaps you're grieving for the positive aspects of the marriage, for instance, and not the negative ones.

Sometimes grief is *delayed* for an extended period of time, which could be months or even years. Why would this happen? It could be because you have an overload of pressing responsibilities. Or perhaps you subconsciously feel you can't deal with the grief right now. When grief over a loss is delayed, some other loss in the future may trigger its release, so the emotions may come like an avalanche. Even a small future loss can be the catalyst to release past grief. Your current loss could do this if you have unresolved grief from a previous circumstance. Or some delay grief because they believe it will go away. Obviously, it doesn't. The grief builds within and typically comes out in a variety of ways that aren't good.

Some people feel that if their grief stays hidden, at some point in time they will be better prepared and feel safer in experiencing the pain. Unaware that through expression comes healing, they may continue to postpone. But grief builds up, pushing to the point of explosion.

This makes it more difficult to experience feelings related to the loss. It is an unfortunate choice for handling grief.

Some spouses experience *conflicted grief*. They exaggerate some of the characteristics of normal grief while blocking other aspects that should also be present. Sometimes in grieving over a loved one, this reaction occurs because of having had either a dependent or ambivalent relationship with your spouse.

Chronic grief is when a spouse continues to exhibit grief responses that were appropriate in the early stages of grief. The mourning continues and doesn't proceed to any sign of closure. You're keeping the loss alive through grief. This is especially prevalent in the loss of a spouse because of the intensity of feelings.[3]

Your Reflections

1. At this time in your grief journey, how are you doing?

2. In what way has your grief been absent?

3. In what way has your grief been minimal?

4. In what way has your grief been inhibiting?

5. In what way has your grief been delayed?

6. In what way has your grief been postponed?

7. In what way has your grief been conflicted?

8. In what way has your grief been chronic?

37

THE LAST TIME WE
WERE TOGETHER

When your spouse dies unexpectedly, the last time you were together is very significant. You remember the last conversation, the last touch, and the surroundings. Everything about that time stands out vividly. It's as though somebody hit a "freeze" button and the movie of your life stopped at that instant. You play it over and over in your mind.

If your last memory was pleasant, grieving is easier. The good memory comforts you. But it doesn't always happen that way. You may have wanted to be with your spouse when he or she died, but the suddenness of the event robbed you of the opportunity. You may have wanted to say more to your mate the last time you were together. Or your last encounter could have been an unpleasant conflict, and the relationship hadn't been fully restored yet. There's a feeling of unfinished business. When you parted you thought, *We'll work this out tonight or tomorrow.* But tomorrow never had a chance to arrive.

The last unpleasant scenes may tend to haunt you. Your task then is to soften the memories and images that hurt you so much. How do you do this? By doing some editing just as if your life is a movie. You can hang on to the hurting, negative images or choose to go back a bit further in time and dwell on a scene that is representative of your overall relationship. That scene can become your source of comfort since it more accurately represents the relationship you had.[1]

Some spouses bypass grieving with *replacement*. You take the emotions that were invested in the relationship that ended in death and prematurely reinvest them in another relationship. For the most part, you may not be conscious that the replacement efforts are really a means of avoiding facing and resolving your grief.

Outsiders sometimes assume the person who is involved so soon must not have loved his or her spouse who died if he or she can so quickly start a new relationship. In actuality, often the replacer has loved very much, and out of the need to overcome the pain of confronting feelings related to the loss, avoids the pain by replacement. Some people who experienced a good marriage may remarry soon because they know the joy of having a quality relationship. Replacement includes a person but can also include excesses, such as overwork or plunging frantically into a hobby.

Your Reflections

1. What was the last statement you made to your spouse?

2. What was the last statement your spouse made to you?

3. Has replacement occurred in your life? If yes, in what ways?

38

THE STRUGGLE OF GRIEF

Why do some spouses move through grief so well while others have such struggles? Are there common clues that can be identified? Yes. There are numerous factors that predispose a person to difficulty in resolving grief over a loss. We have to allow for variations of responses in grief, but for now let's consider recognizable unresolved grief.

One reason unresolved grief occurs is because a spouse is unable to handle the emotional pain. You may resist the process, causing delays. Or it could be that you have an excessive need to maintain interaction with the spouse who is no longer available. It's a struggle to admit the other person is really gone.

Guilt can block grief. If you reflect on your relationship with your spouse who is gone, you may experience excessive guilt over behaviors, feelings, or even issues such as neglect that may have occurred in the relationship. If you have high standards regarding interpersonal relationships, it may not take too much to activate your guilt. This in turn blocks the grieving, since you feel unable to confront the guilt.

You may also struggle with "survivor guilt." When I was conducting a Grief Recovery Seminar on Long Island in New York following the September 11, 2001 tragedy, a mother shared that her son had worked at Cantor Fitzgerald, a company that lost several hundred employees. A friend and another fellow employee asked her son to take off Tuesday and Wednesday of that week to go on a fishing trip. Her son declined because he was taking Monday off to play in a company golf tournament and didn't want to be away from work too much. So the other two employees took the day off while her son went to work and was killed. Just imagine the "what ifs" that run through this mother's mind and the survivor guilt the two friends may experience. Both can block recovery.

Have you heard someone say, "My life is a total loss without her. I feel like half a person. I can't function without him (or her)"? This could reflect excessive dependence, that in turn leads to an avoidance of grieving. You try to void the reality of the loss because part of the loss seems to be in you.

Some resist grieving because the loss reactivates unresolved losses from the past that are even more painful to handle than the present one. An endless pattern of postponing grieving is set into motion.

Overload may be another reason for unresolved grief. There are occasions in our lives when we experience a number of losses in a short period of time, and it's just too much pain to bear and process at one time. The losses are too heavy to face and handle. If you lost several members of your family or even several friends at one time, it produces overload and you've lost some of the people who may have offered you support and comfort as you grieve.

Still others fail to grieve because of errors of beliefs. For instance, you may fear losing control because you've been taught that losing control isn't proper. You don't want to appear weak. Or maybe you don't want to give up your pain because it ties you closer to the person you lost.

Your Reflections

1. Which of the reasons for unresolved grief do you relate to most?

2. If you identified with any of these, what can you do to move ahead?

39

TAKE TIME

If you found yourself in the last few pages, here are some doable suggestions.

Identify what doesn't make sense to you about the loss of your spouse. Perhaps there's a vague question about life or God's purpose for you. Or it could be a specific question: "Why did this have to happen to me now, at this crucial point in my life?" Ask, "What is bothering me the most?" Keep a small card or notebook with you for several days so you can record your thoughts as they emerge.

Identify the emotions you feel during each day. Are you experiencing sadness, anger, regret, "if onlys," hurt, or guilt? What or who are the feelings directed at? Has the intensity of the feelings decreased or increased during the past few days? If your feelings are vague, identifying and labeling them will diminish their power over you.

State the steps or actions you are taking to help you move ahead. Identify what you have done in the past that has helped. Ask a trusted friend for help.

Share your loss and grief with others who will listen to you and support you. Don't seek advice-givers, but find those friends who are empathetic and can handle your feelings. Remember, your journey through grief will not be exactly like that of another person. Each of us is unique, so don't compare your grief with others' feelings.

Find a person who has experienced a similar loss. Groups and organizations abound for losses of all types. Reading books or stories about those who have survived similar experiences may be helpful. Many find support through websites of various organizations.

Identify the positive characteristics and strengths of your life that helped you before. Which of these will help you at this time in your life?

Spend time reading in the book of Psalms. Many psalms reflect the struggle of human loss and offer the comfort and assurance that come from God's mercies. (I also recommend reading *The North Face of God* by Ken Gire.)

Share your confusion, your feelings, and your hopes with God. Even if you're angry with God, sharing your protest is an act of faith and belief. Stay involved in the worship services of your church because worship is an important element in recovery and stabilization. (Read *A Sacred Sorrow* by Michael Card.)

Think about where you want to be two years from now. Write out some of your dreams and goals. Setting some goals may encourage you to realize you will recover.

Become familiar with the process of grief. Knowing what to expect helps you not be thrown by what you're experiencing or will experience.

Remember that understanding your grief intellectually isn't enough. It can't replace the emotional experience of living through this difficult time. You need to be patient and allow your feelings to catch up with your mind. Expect mood swings. They are normal! Remind yourself of the grief process through notes placed in obvious places.

My Journal

Sitting at the piano. I thought today would be different. I hoped to get through the hours with a sense of calm and stability, but it wasn't to be. I started completing Joyce's book she started in 2001 to give to Sheryl. This was more difficult than I thought. Then I found one of the many hymns Joyce's mom wrote. I sat down at the piano and played it. It sounded just like something Joyce would have written. I move on to two other pieces I used to play while Joyce prepared dinner in the kitchen. Sometimes as I play I expect her to walk in silently and sit either at the table or behind me on the couch like she used to do. I catch myself looking toward the kitchen now and then, but all I see are one or both cats stretched out with contented looks on their faces…hopefully enjoying the music. Perhaps they really do, for they come walking into the room each evening when I begin to play. They are a source of comfort.

Once or twice a week I play the song that was the background music at Joyce's memorial service. It draws me closer to her because in my mind I can see the photos displayed there. When I play I still have something of Joyce. I hope it's always that way.

Your Reflections

1. What days have been better for you, and why?

2. Which days have been the most difficult, and why?

40

Moving On

Life is full of moving days. The van drives up to the house, and the neighbor's furniture is loaded. The goodbyes are said, and the neighbors wave and slowly diminish in size as their vehicles move down the street. One location is left behind, and a new one awaits. Perhaps there's sorrow over what is left and anticipation over what's ahead. Moving days are part of life...and sometimes it's because of death.

My Journal

Moving day. September 15—a day to remember—moving day. I remember when we moved into this house on Thanksgiving of 2002. The house had been empty, but we soon filled it with boxes and furniture and people and pets. Soon the house became a home. But today someone moved out. Joyce received an invitation to a new residence. She received a better offer, one without cancerous tumors or pain.

She moved sooner than anyone expected...or...wanted for that matter. It's true we can be glad for her new life and new body and new residence in heaven. But that doesn't make it any easier. God had a different timetable for Joyce. He's in charge of that part of our lives; we aren't. We don't understand the timing nor do we need to. My heart is different now that Joyce has moved out and left empty spots in my life.

Her La-Z-Boy chair sits quiet and empty, save for the cat who hops up to sleep there on occasion.

Her spot in the bed is empty and the covers on her side are unruffled.

Her footsteps as she walked through the house are strangely missing.

The refrigerator door and cupboards remain closed most of the time.

The sounds of preparation for church on Sunday have been silenced, and the question heard for decades on Sunday mornings, "Now, what time are we leaving?" has been silenced.

How strange it is that the sounds of silence seem louder than the roar of a waterfall. That is what I hear and feel in my home—silence where there was once sound, emptiness where there was once presence.

I miss her eyes. They were eyes that spoke with compassion, conviction, and love. There was a sparkle. They brought joy to others. But in the last days, they seemed silent, staring, searching. I wish I knew what they were saying and searching for. I wonder what they were seeing or not seeing. Was anything registering? Were they wandering as her mind was? I asked, "What can you see?" but I received no response.

The most difficult times were the tearful eyes. The bits of moisture that gathered at the corner of her eyes left me wondering and searching. "What do you need?" I asked. "What can I do? How can I help you?" Questions and puzzlement were my companions. I so wanted to help her. There was a message in those tears, but I couldn't decipher the meaning. The helpless feeling that comes with the inability to help and to serve when a loved one is suffering is a terrible experience. I felt as though I couldn't come through when I was needed. I failed.

And then on the last days her eyes were silent. They weren't talking anymore. The eyelids were down as though frozen shut. There was no movement as though her eyes were tired and ready to close forever.

And so now one has moved on and one remains. The struggle is how to move forward through the residual left behind that is called grief. So many spouses feel incomplete. "There was so much I wanted to say," they admit. "There was so much I wanted to hear my spouse say to me," they share. I can relate.

Your Reflections

1. What are several things you miss the most at this time?

2. What would you say to your spouse if you had the opportunity?

MAKING AMENDS

No marriage is perfect. It's a constant process of growth. A marriage doesn't demand perfection. What is needed is priority. As one friend said, "It's an institution for sinners, and no one else need apply. And it finds its finest glory when we sinners see it as God's way of leading us through his ultimate curriculum of love and righteousness."

Some people lose their partners at a time when their marriages are rich and fulfilling. Others, however, lose their spouses when their unions are troubled and distant. But no matter what the state the marriage is in, death hurts.

What do you do with unresolved tensions and issues? How do you deal with the abundance of regrets and if onlys? There are some steps you can take to move on after the death of your loved one. The first is very simple. It's making amends. Making amends is not just saying you're sorry for what you regret. It's also about changing your responses. Ask, "What positive or negative events or situations did I not make amends for?" You can be sorry for something you did or for something you wished you'd done or said.

What Can You Do?

If there was a negative response, something you wish you could have changed earlier, what can you do about it now? One widow said, "I wish I'd been less negative and critical and been more verbally appreciative. Now I'm making sure that I give two or three affirmations or compliments for every criticism or concern I express." There is sorrow but also positive change.

Another said, "I wish I had told him more often how special he was to me. At least I've started doing this more with other people now."

It's important to remember this about forgiveness: It's a process and can take time. Forgiveness means we will not blame or hold something against ourselves or our spouses anymore.

The second step is identifying those areas where forgiveness is needed. Many struggle with this, and there are many reasons for not forgiving.

Your Reflections

1. What are your regrets and if onlys?

2. Can you identify some areas of difficulty in forgiving that you experience?

It's important to identify the reasons behind not forgiving. Write your spouse's name on top of a piece of paper. Below his or her name write a salutation like in a letter. Under the salutation write, "I forgive you for..." and complete the sentence by writing down everything that has bothered you over the years. Try to capture the immediate thoughts that come to your mind after writing your statement of forgiveness. It might be a rebuttal or objection to forgiving the other person. Write the statement opposite the "I forgive you" statement.

Continue the exercise by writing "I forgive you" statements followed by your first thoughts—even if they are contradictory. Repeat the process until you have drained *all* your pockets of resentment. When you come to a place where you can write "I forgive you" several times with no objections or rebuttals, you've let go and forgiveness is occurring. Whether a person is living or deceased, forgiveness does more for you than for him or her.

A final step involves significant emotional statements that usually involve statements you wish you could have said. Many of us long for one more conversation with our spouses. Some of the following sentence starters may help you. Ask, "If I could complete these statements to my spouse, what would they be?" Statements could include:

- I appreciate you for...
- I was so proud of you for...
- It meant so much to me...
- Thank you for...
- You were so special at...

Some people have also found it helpful to recall the last conversation with their spouses and then share what they remember.

At the conclusion of completing this exercise, you may want to say goodbye. This may involve every aspect of your relationship, including goodbyes to emotional and physical incompletenesses, pain, and lack of forgiveness.

42

LETTING GO

Another variation of the steps described in the preceding chapter is writing a "Letting Go" letter. Here is an example to guide you.

Dear Honey,

Your death has left a gaping hole in my life and heart, producing an emptiness I know will never be filled. I miss your voice, the sound of your laughter, those funny endearing things you did, and those moments when I was infuriated at you. I miss the dreams I had for and with you. I miss the future we will never have and the past which, no matter how long it may have been, will never be long enough.

I have wept for you as well as for myself. I have raged in anger at you, at God, at the world, at anyone and anything that seemed to be an appropriate target. I have tried to understand why you are no longer with me, and why I have to struggle through this world without you. Some people have reached out to help me; others have turned away, unable to bear the pain I carry. I do not ask them to share it with me, only to listen as I talk and cry. I have waited in the darkness for some sign that you are in a better, safer place, and even when I may have received it, I couldn't help but question how it could be better if I'm not there with you. I have wanted to join you so often, especially when the aloneness threatens to overwhelm me.

Through all of this turmoil and doubt, I've managed to come this far. I have not yet achieved my goal, but at least I can now recognize that I am on the road to recovery. I am not sure how I will go on without you. No matter how many other important people may be in my life, you always held a special place, and it is hard to imagine you not with me.

I can't come to you at this time. I can only trust that we will be reunited in God's love and compassion in heaven.

My life must go on. It is time for me to begin to live my life for myself and others.

I'm letting you go. I know you will never leave my heart. Thank you for the wonderful, unique relationship we shared. When we meet once more, I look forward to sharing my new experiences with you. I love you. I miss you. I will never forget you.

Your Reflections

1. If you were to write such a letter what would you say?

FIGHTING YOUR GRIEF

There are many who resist, fight, or even hate their grief. This too is normal. But just as in heart surgery, some people would like to have a grief bypass.

"Communicating with Your Grief" will be a helpful experience for you. This is one way for you to take charge of your grieving process.[1] This experience dispels the notion that grief is a six-headed monster that will get you if you mention its name. This is an opportunity to communicate with your grief as though it has a personality of its own. You will talk to your grief, and you will also listen to your grief.

Letter #1

You will be writing two letters. Use stationery you normally use for writing to family or friends. The first letter is from you to your grief. Use this form:

Date _____ Time _____

To Grief,

Text

Sincerely,

Before you start to write, ask, "If I could tell my grief what I am thinking and feeling, what would I say? What do I want my grief to know about its impact on my life?" Now be as frank as you can and write your letter. Don't forget to sign it.

Here is an example of the first letter.

Dear Grief,

You are a rascal. You take our energy, our organizational abilities, our brains and do strange things with them. I was prepared for the immediate grief and to feel the loss of my spouse for a long, long time. I was not prepared for the laziness, low energy level, and stress.

I'm impatient with it all. You take so much out of us when we really need to be able to function well.

I must confess, though, that you've done good things for me. I am more compassionate, understanding, and tolerant now. You have given me new ways to be of service, and God will show me what to do. Perhaps after I've had more time to look back, I'll feel differently about you, but for right now you are not one of my favorite friends. But I am a better person because of you, and I must not lose sight of that.

> Sincerely,
> Irene

Letter #2

Approximately 24 hours later (no less than that) write a second letter. This one will be *from* your grief to you. Use the same format as the first letter except address it to yourself and sign it "Sincerely, Grief." Before writing, ask, "What do I think my grief is telling me? What does it want from me?" As frankly as possible, write to yourself on behalf of your grief.

Here is the second letter Irene wrote the day after she wrote to grief.

Dear Irene,

I'm sorry I've caused you so much pain. Remember what your pastor said at the funeral? "Grief is the noblest emotion of all." It truly is the last gift of love you can give to your husband. So experience it in a normal way. Let your own time frame happen. I know you are working hard to get through this phase of your life. I commend you for that. But I also want to say "Let go and let God." Just put your life in God's hands. I suggest you read the verses on death in God's Word. Remember, there is an atomic bomb of hope waiting to explode between the front and back covers of your Bible. I sense the excitement you'll feel as you search through those Scriptures. You may be truly amazed at what you find.

Begin to use your time more wisely. Get extra sleep once or twice a week. You'll be all right. Soon your energy level will return. You may even lose the weight you've been trying to get rid of. In time you'll walk lighter. You will be lighter. You'll feel great.

I am your friend. I am a part of life. There is a purpose for me. You will see.

> Sincerely,
> Grief

The Next Step

Put the letters aside for a day or two, and then read them both out loud to yourself. What do they reveal about your attitude toward the experience of grief? What new things do you learn about yourself from your letters?

Find someone with whom you can share the letters and talk about your discoveries. If you're in a grief support group, this is an excellent activity to share with one another.

Your Reflections

1. What are your thoughts about grief?

HELPING OTHERS HELP YOU

Too often others don't know how to respond to or what to say about your loss. Unfortunately, we get to educate them on grief and what will help us and comfort us in the midst of our grief.

One creative way of letting others know about your situation is through a weekly update on your answering machine. A widower I counseled for two years shared this experience with me. He continued these answering machine messages over a period of four years and transcribed each one so he would have a written record of his grief journey. Many friends would purposely call when he was at work to get the weekly update and not intrude or disturb him. This was his way of letting others know how to pray for him. It also helped to answer his adult daughter's questions and brought a new closeness to his family. Here's an example of three messages from him after his wife died of cancer.

> March 7, 1997
>
> Hi, this is Dave.
>
> I'm feeling overwhelmed and lost. I'm feeling the great loss of all the dreams Irene and I have worked for over the years... now gone. My fear of the future is like a deep, sharp pain. I wasn't ready for this to happen. Please pray that we can do what it says in Proverbs 3:5-6: "Trust in the LORD with all your heart and lean not on your own understanding; in all your ways acknowledge him, and he will make your paths straight."

April 19, 1997

It's been five months since I've been able to really hold Irene in my arms and hug her. There were many times after her surgery when I wanted to comfort her with a hug. But all I could do was hold her hand and rearrange her pillows into a different position for her. I feel great loss, and I'm really sad about that.

I know there are others who are in stressful circumstances and relationships. So if you'll leave your name, I'll pray for you. I'm reminded of what God said through Isaiah about comfort for his people: "Do you not know? Have you not heard? The LORD is the everlasting God, the Creator of the ends of the earth. He will not grow tired or weary, and his understanding no one can fathom. He gives strength to the weary and increases the power of the weak" (Isaiah 40:28-29).

August 12, 1997

Hi, this is Dave.

I'm having lots of ugly thoughts and worldly feelings, and I'm filled with shame because I struggle with taking them to the Lord and leaving them at the foot of the cross.

So my prayer request is to help me remember the words of the psalmist: "The LORD is gracious and compassionate, slow to anger and rich in love. The LORD is good to all; he has compassion on all he has made" (Psalm 145:8-9).[1]

One of the best steps to take to help others respond to you is constructing an explanation letter and sharing it at work and elsewhere:

Dear Friends (family, pastor, fellow workers),

Recently I've suffered a devastating loss. I am grieving, and it will take months and even years to recover.

I want you to know that I will cry from time to time. I don't apologize for my tears since they are not a sign of weakness or a lack of faith. They are God's gift to me to express the extent of my loss, and they are also a sign that I am recovering.

At times you may see me angry for no apparent reason. Sometimes I'm not sure why. All I know is that my emotions are intense because of my grief. If I don't always make sense to you, please be forgiving and patient with me. And if I repeat myself again and again, please accept this as normal.

More than anything else, I need your understanding and your presence. You don't always have to know what to say... or even to say anything if you don't know how to respond. Your presence and a touch or hug lets me know you care. Please don't wait for me to call you since sometimes I am too tired or tearful to do so.

If I tend to withdraw from you, please don't let me do that. I need you to reach out to me for the next several months.

Pray for me that I will come to see meaning in my loss someday and that I will know God's comfort and love. It does help to let me know you are praying for me.

If you have experienced a similar type of loss, please feel free to share it with me. It will help rather than cause me to feel worse. And don't stop sharing if I begin to cry. It's all right. Any tears you shed as we talk are all right too.

This loss is so painful, and right now it feels like the worst thing that could ever happen to me. But I will survive and eventually recover. I cling to that knowledge, even though there have been times when I didn't feel it. I know that I will not always feel as I do now. Laughter and joy will emerge once again someday.

There are words in our language that can be used somewhat lightly. That is, until you lose your spouse. Then they become words that identify and haunt...like "alone" and "incomplete." These common thoughts and common feelings that describe a new and undesired journey.

Thank you for caring about me. Thank you for listening and praying. Your concern comforts me and is a gift I will always cherish.[2]

Returning to a job after a spouse's death is a step that tends to be anticipated with eagerness, dread, or both, at different times. The workplace can seem like a familiar well-ordered refuge where you find many hours of distraction from your pain. On the other hand, it can represent the ordeal of work pressure, coworker reactions, and unrealistic expectations from management.

How can you make it through a workday while you're grieving?

- While your private world has been drastically changed, your workplace has gone along in its usual way. You may, therefore, initially feel out of sync with the rest of your coworkers.

- Coworkers will look to you for their cue. Others usually feel awkward about expressing feelings or knowing the "right thing" to say. How you respond to the first expressions of sympathy will convey a message to other coworkers about how and if you want to deal with the loss. Some possible responses include: "Thank you. It's difficult to talk right now. Maybe later" or "I appreciate your concern." Remember, the choice is yours.

- Some coworkers may not mention the loss. This can feel painful and even insulting. Try to bear in mind that people are often afraid of "reminding" or "upsetting" a grieving person. Expressing sadness can seem especially threatening in a work setting, where personal distress is supposed to take a backseat to the demands of business.

- Be prepared for unexpected tears. During the first weeks back at work there may be moments you find yourself tearful. This will get better with time, but for now, give yourself permission to retreat to the restroom or another secluded area for a good cry or to compose yourself. Many find giving themselves this "release" helps relieve the pressure of having to control feelings of grief while at work.

- Be prepared to experience some difficulty with memory and

concentration. Remember, these are common but *temporary* symptoms of grief. While you may feel frustrated and anxious about this change, try to be patient with yourself. It helps to reread and/or go over information or tasks more than once.

- Your boss or coworkers may have unrealistic expectations. Assure them you're doing your best, and that any slowdown on your part is temporary.

- Despite how others may react, it is important for you to recognize that what is going on is normal and temporary. With time and patience (especially your own), you will regain the capacity you used to have to do your job.[3]

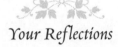

Your Reflections

1. If you were to compose a letter to give to others, what would you say?

2. Who could help you write this letter?

45

REMEMBRANCE

In this unwanted journey of losing your spouse you have such a jumble of thoughts and feelings. Do they make sense? Not always. We live for weeks or months or even years wanting to retrieve the person taken from us. We often exist in a state of longing. And each memory experience seems to come when we least expect it. This was mine.

My Journal

Longing. I was sitting at my desk listening to a new Jim Brickman CD entitled "Hope" that someone gave me. I've played most of his songs on the piano, and many were Joyce's favorites. When I played she would slip in behind me sometimes and sit on the couch to watch and listen. I was overly critical of my playing but she was completely appreciative. Music had always brought us closer together without us having to say much about it.

As I listened to the song "Longing," it dawned on me, "This would have been one of Joyce's favorites. *Longing*—a feeling of desire for something unobtainable. It's a beautiful, gentle, delicate melody with a few minor twists that are very unsettling. This too reflects a sense of longing. It's a reflective tune—the type she always liked. It's slow with expressive pauses, and then for a few measures it's definite, as if making a statement of longing.

Joyce, I wish I could play it for you and send it to heaven so we could be connected again. And perhaps another reason I'm so moved by this piece is its name, for I long to see you, hear you, touch you, walk with you, sit next to you, and just have more time with you. My own sense of longing is intense. But I guess that will have to wait for a while. And as painful as the longing is at times, I never want to lose that sense. And how can it be lost when over 70 percent of my life was spent with you?

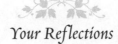

Your Reflections

1. When are the times you long for your spouse the most?

2. What do you long for?

3. Does it change or is it always the same?

46

Surprises from God

Sometimes God surprises us in the midst of our struggles. He did me.

I heard Joyce sing again. I was standing in the kitchen talking to Gary on the phone. We were asking one another how our Christmas went, in spite of both of us being without our wives for the first time. We shared what we did as well as the strangeness of being without the one we loved most. Gary talked about going to the places where he and Carrie used to go and mentioned he wished he could call her and have just one more conversation with her. He wanted to hear her voice one more time, just as I wanted to hear Joyce's voice again. I said, "That's why I put on videos of her—to hear and see her—but it's not the same." We both agreed it's not going to happen here, but it will happen in the future, in heaven.

We talked more and he asked what time of the day was the worst for me. It made me stop and think. There is no pattern. There is no predictability. It varies, with some days more intense than others, but sometimes it is up to me, depending on where I allow my mind to go. If I envision Joyce during the last days as she was dying, the waves of grief begin to roll. It will probably take some time before the images of her living override those of death.

Why do we dream what we dream? I'm not sure. But that same

night I dreamed Joyce and I were in a large room. A woman was at a piano singing, not to the sound of the piano but to another accompaniment such as a CD. The woman stopped. Joyce began to sing in her soft, beautiful voice…just as I used to hear her sing around the house. I was hearing Joyce sing again! It was so different than other dreams because it was so vivid, so real. I realize now this dream was a gift. I woke up with silent sobs. I wanted to return to the dream, but I couldn't. I wish I could have taped my dream to retain what I'd experienced. Where so many of my dreams fade away within minutes, this one stayed with visual and auditory clarity long enough for me to write and capture it as best I could. I can still see and hear the experience. It was wonderful.

Joyce continues to sing in my mind and my memories. But she's also singing somewhere else continually as she voices praises to our King in glory. Hallelujah and amen.

Your Reflections

1. What I miss the most is…

2. What I would like to experience again is…

3. The dreams I've had of my spouse are…

4. The dreams I would like to have are…

47

What I'd Like to Say

I talked with a friend of mine who recently lost her husband. She told me what she missed most were the conversations. They'd seemed to talk constantly no matter where they were. And it's true—the one we could share with, talk to, and listen to is gone. What we want to say or may even begin to say is still there but once again we're without. What is it like?

My Journal

If you were here I would tell you... There are so many times when I need to talk with you. Tonight was one of them. I needed to hear your voice and its reassuring tone. I needed to see your face and the sparkle in your eye and to hold your hand. As I walked Shadow I thought of what I wished I could tell you.

I would tell you...

> ...I'm reading as much as I can about heaven to find out what I can expect when I finally arrive and what you've already discovered. I want to know what is true about heaven rather than the wishful thinking of others.

> ...that you would be pleasantly surprised and pleased with how loving and responsive Misty Blue Bell has become. She's become the cat you wanted her to be, and that's so important because I remember the look on your face when you first held her at the cattery.

...about the people who are making trips up here to see me and spend time just sitting and sharing. How special this is.

...The other morning I read words from a woman who experienced cancer as you did, and perhaps you've already met her there. She said, "Embrace life, go after your dreams, but learn that each moment with loved ones is the most wonderful thing life has to offer." So times with others have become the most important parts of daily life.

...that you trained me well. I follow routines that you instilled within me as if you were still here. You are still here and always will be.

...that you have no idea (or maybe you do now) how you impacted so many people by your example, your spirit, and your love. And you did this without many words either.

...about the new flowers in the backyard. They're a soft, delicate blue color, which reminds me of you. They're delphiniums but not the usual ones. You would have sat there and gazed upon them, enjoying the color as you often did.

...about Colleen's dog who ate a bar of soap and was soon blowing soap bubbles all over the house, but from the wrong end! She said it was a mess, but my response was, "Your dog just left you with a great memory as well as something else!" You know me...always looking at the positive side of life. That's still there except in not having you here anymore. I wish you were by my side again.

...the last two days have been really emotional. I feel a constant state of sadness. I'm missing seeing you and hearing your voice. It's like I'm living in a house with a great chasm, and I find my tears are just an inch below the surface.

...about your pine tree next to the driveway, the one you wanted trimmed. You would love the way it looks. I had the man trim it the way you would have liked it, more severe than my preference, but had you been here it would have been this way. I've realized that over the years my first response so often changed to line up with what you wanted anyway. And that was good. I just wish for more of those opportunities.

...about Grandparent's Day. I needed you there. I wanted you to see your granddaughter up on the stage. She was having so much fun with all the people and attention. Then the principal asked each of the eight children what they called their grandmother. When Shaelyn was asked, she hesitated for a moment as if she were stumped by the questions. For a moment she was at a rare loss for words and then she said, "PapaSan." I guess it was because you and Evelyn are gone, and I'm the only one left. The vacancy in our lives raises its presence everywhere and at anytime. And today it will be felt again since it's Shaelyn's sixth birthday. I remember the chaos of the last one when the piñata seemed to be made of cast iron steel and wouldn't break. The large doll with the black hair that you wanted her to have someday will become a part of her life now.

Your Reflections

1. What would you like to tell your spouse at this time?

48

CAREGIVER—A PRIVILEGE

Scripture calls us to encourage one another and to bear one another's burdens. Caring for a spouse during their last days is the ultimate expression of this calling. It's a task we never imagined having to do or wanting to be part of our lives.

You may have been a caregiver. If so, you went through a difficult ordeal, for watching a loved one suffer or just linger can be painful. You feel so helpless as you watch the physical and mental changes become evident as the disease takes its toll. Your mate's facial expressions may have changed. Perhaps you saw the gradual loss of recognition of people and surroundings. Each change is a loss for your spouse... and for you. It's like saying goodbye to him or her piece by piece. If this happened to you, it's important to revisit the experience to make peace with its existence. Let's consider your daily routine prior to your spouse dying.

1. What time did you get up in the morning?

2. Did you have coffee or breakfast with your spouse?

3. Did you talk or have devotions together?

4. Did your spouse go to work? If so, at what time?

5. Did you go to work? If so, what time did you leave?

6. If you didn't work outside the home, what activities did you do during the day (go to the gym, have lunch with friends, volunteer, housework)? Did you do any of these together?

7. Did you and your spouse see each other in the evening?

8. Who prepared meals, and who cleaned up?

9. What time did you eat together?

10. Did you watch TV together? What programs?

11. Did you sleep together in the same bed?

12. Did you spend weekends and holidays together?

13. Did you spend summers together?

14. Did you vacation together? What did you like to do and where?

15. Did you have favorite vacation spots you visited at special times?

Likely, all of these activities helped define the structure of your day, your week, your month, and your year. But now that your spouse is gone, the structure of your life has changed.

Now, pick a period of time after your spouse died and answer these questions.

1. What time do you get up in the morning?

2. Do you go out for coffee or breakfast or eat at home?

3. How do you spend your day? At work? Doing volunteer activities? Exercising?

4. Do you see friends during these activities?

5. What do you do for dinner in the evening? Do you eat alone? At home? Do you cook?

6. What do you do after dinner? Watch TV? If so, do you watch alone? Do you watch the same shows you watched or do the same evening activities you did when your spouse was alive?

7. How do you end your evening (call your adult children, read, go to sleep in a different bed from the one you slept in when your spouse was alive)?

8. How do you spend your time on weekends?

9. How do you spend your holidays?

10. What do you do for vacations? Or what do you think you will do?

11. How do these vacation activities differ from what you did while your spouse was alive?

Compare your answers to the first and second set of questions. How many of the daily activities are different from those you engaged in when your spouse was alive?[1] You may want to revisit these questions six months from now.

49

ANTICIPATORY GRIEVING

When we're caregivers, our grieving often begins with the first serious symptoms of our spouse's diseases and/or the diagnosis. Part of us doesn't want to believe the worst, and yet part of us does believe. The grief grows the more we learn to grieve.

As your spouse deteriorated, your grief probably intensified, but sometimes you were so busy you weren't aware of the grieving. This happened to me. For two years I grieved but was so preoccupied with helping Joyce that it went unnoticed. It was later that I fully realized how much grief I was in during that time.

For some, this "anticipatory grief" may shorten the grief journey that occurs after the death of the loved one. For others, it may have less effect or no effect at all.[1]

My Journal

Loss is no stranger. I called a friend the other night. Part of me didn't want to make the call. It was a difficult one. It was hard but necessary. He had called and left a message wishing Joyce and me a blessed Christmas. He must not have received my emails about Joyce. I tracked down his number and called. When I asked if he'd received my messages the last few months he said no. I paused, struggling with my emotions as well as with how to tell him. After a few seconds I heard him say in a soft voice, "I think I know what you're going to tell me." And then I did. I got it out. And he understood for he too had lost his wife. That was about 15 years ago. His current wife is almost bedridden with fibromyalgia.

During the conversation I mentioned that in the year prior to Joyce's death I felt I was losing the Joyce I'd known. And his description was so apt, "The Joyce you knew was disappearing in front of you." That was so true. With certain types of illnesses loved ones gradually disappear in front of our eyes. They fade from the people they once were. We live with an ongoing loss. Joyce and I did that together with our son, Matthew. Loss wasn't a stranger that visited now and then. It became a permanent resident in our lives.

Juggling as Best You Can

If you were a caregiver, perhaps you haven't yet fully realized what you experienced during this time and how it may be contributing to your grief. You may have felt like a juggler trying to keep the demands of other family members, your job, and the time you wanted to spend with your dying spouse all up in the air and moving at once. When you faced these demands you probably often neglected your own well-being.

Did you feel out of control over the sudden and unexpected events that occurred, including the changes in your spouse's condition?

And then there is the physical exhaustion you incurred, which could be continuing. Perhaps all you did during that time is but a blur now and something you'd like to forget.

Many people discover after their spouses died that the financial stability they thought they had evaporated due to all the medical and related expenses. And at a time when it's hard to concentrate, difficult decisions need to be made.

As if all this isn't enough, you may have to deal with other family members. Perhaps there were some who were more conspicuous by their absence than their presence. Did this happen to you? Did you struggle with, "Where were they when I needed them?" Or you may have those who wanted to do too much or wanted more control over decisions and disagreed with your decisions. Perhaps others offered too many suggestions or wondered how your dying spouse would affect them financially. Maybe relatives on your spouse's side of the family had strong ideas on the funeral arrangements or location for burial. All these added to your grief.

You also may not have taken care of yourself at this time—physically, emotionally, or spiritually. You cared for your spouse and other family members, perhaps not even having leftover time for your own health and self-care.

And then came the pressures of end-of-life responsibilities. Some struggle with location—home versus rest home versus hospital. Or did you have to make the decision about the machines—to leave them on or turn them off. For some this prompts second guessing and guilt. Many people wish they didn't have to be the primary ones making all these critical, major decisions.

You may not even like who you became during this time. Emotional erosion is so common that friends may even say you're not yourself. And that's true. You couldn't be at this time because even before your spouse died you were grieving. Your patience may have worn thin and for good reason. Physical exhaustion leads to emotional exhaustion.

Your Reflections

1. What did you learn about yourself during this time of care giving?

2. What do you need to do for you at this time in your life?

50

WONDERING

One of the greatest gifts we've received from God is our mind—our abilities to think and imagine. Being creative and resourceful lets us move forward in life. But imagination can also be one of the greatest sources of pain because of what we choose to dwell on. What we think about and say to ourselves feeds our emotions and our grief. Imagination is to our emotions what illustrations are to a text or music is to a love story.

Often we fixate on thoughts and questions that plague the pathways of our minds. Have you gotten stuck on an image?

I Wonder...

Do you ever wonder what goes through the mind of others? I have. I still do...and especially about Joyce during her last weeks of life. This makes me wonder what I would think and feel if I were in her circumstance and place in life. I wonder what I *will* think and feel when it is my time to die. At 70, and because Joyce is gone, that is much more real than ever before. I see it less as an ending and more as a transition, a beginning in a new life. The hundreds of cards and emails I've received in the past month have this consistent theme too, which leads me to a sense of comfort and reassurance. But every now and then I still wonder...

> ...what went through Joyce's mind each morning when she woke, knowing there was a sleeping enemy within her head that could awaken at anytime...and eventually did.

...how much of her thoughts and feelings were for herself or for what this was doing to her loved ones in her life. And knowing Joyce as I did, I think I know because she cared so much for others.

...what she experienced when she asked, "How long?" and heard "It could be two weeks or a month or two." What is it like when you're told the news and then experience the process slowly as symptoms intensify and your words and thoughts diminish? And what frustration it must be to think you've said something clearly only to see puzzlement on the faces of others and realize you didn't say what you thought you did.

...did the pain and discomfort at the end overshadow looking forward to going to heaven? Could she remember the comfort of Scripture? Could she remember and hear and feel our expressions of love? I hope so.

I have a number of other wondrous thoughts. But they will remain in this state, at least for now.

Finally, brothers, whatever is true, whatever is noble, whatever is right, whatever is pure, whatever is lovely, whatever is admirable—if anything is excellent or praiseworthy—think about such things (Philippians 4:8).

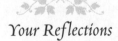

Your Reflections

1. What did you wonder about in your spouse's life and decline?

2. What thoughts would you like to have more control over right now?

51

Who Am I Now?

Who am I now? This is an underlying question most of us confront when our spouses die. We are not the same. We've changed.

Your spouse's death caused a massive shift in what you did, what you will do, and who you are for now. You are no longer part of a couple. The more your life revolved around being married, the greater your discomfort will be. Your roles are now different as are your responsibilities. Your "label," for lack of a better word, is different. Your time, energy, and focus are now different.

If you were focusing on your spouse and his or her needs more than yourself, you may feel even more adrift and fragmented. What to do about all you used to do is a dilemma. It may be difficult to take the step that's necessary at this time—focusing on and taking care of you. And it's not just who you are now, but it also includes who you want to be in the future.

You may not feel there is a future, but there will…and you have a hand in shaping it. At this point in time it may be overwhelming just to get through the day let alone consider next month or next year. But at some point you will. And as you do, enlist the help of others who are wise, compassionate, and supportive to assist you. Just as we don't want to grieve in isolation, it is best to enlist others in planning for your future. The wisdom and knowledge found in Scripture can help us grasp the hope of a future.

> "For I know the plans I have for you," declares the LORD,
> "plans to prosper you and not to harm you, plans to give you
> hope and a future" (Jeremiah 29:11).

Call to me [the LORD] and I will answer you and tell you great
and unsearchable things you do not know (Jeremiah 33:3).

We won't be the same person three months, six months, or a year
or two from now. And we don't move forward *when* the grief is concluded but *while* it is present. Some of us will go in and out of grief
for years even when we've built an entirely new life. That is normal.
What you do with your time, energy, resources, heart, and mind will
be different. (And if you could foresee the future, you would probably
be surprised at how active and involved your life will be.)

Your Reflections

1. What are your thoughts about your future?

2. What plans would you like to make for your future?

52

THE IMPORTANCE OF GOODBYE

Goodbyes are difficult. Even in the happiest of times and the best of circumstances we are hesitant. Often we say the word and then talk a bit more and then say goodbye again. We don't want the contact to end, for when we part there is a sense of aloneness.

My Journal

A whisper of absence. The house is quiet. Oh, there are some sounds and a few noises now and then. But it's not the same. I make some noise as I do activities and conduct business, but it doesn't always cut the silence of Joyce's absence. Her absence is a hovering, invisible cloud or a prevailing sense of a different atmosphere that is transient...but I have no idea what the outcome will be when it settles. Perhaps I don't really want to know the outcome. Or it could be just a small part of me does. I know there's a cloud over the future. And the future isn't something a 70-year-old often considers. It feels strange to see the number 70 in print and realize it's written by me and in reference to me! The cloud isn't there because I'm wondering how many years I have or the quality of health I may have or if I'll always have my wits intact. It's asking, Will this really change or in 10 years will I be as I am this evening? Thoughts come and go. And when I walk through the door, sometimes it's almost like I hear a "whisper." That's such a common word nowadays. We have the "dog whisperer," the "ghost whisperer," the "horse whisperer." But now and then I hear a whisper of absence in the house as well as in my life. And this whisperer brings a feeling of loneliness to the house. And it's not the fault of the house. It's comfortable, spacious, warm, and inviting. It's the presence of grief and your absence, Joyce. That's the whisper. God's Word draws me back into hope, and for that I am thankful. "Weeping may remain for a night, but rejoicing comes in the morning" (Psalm 30:5).

The finality of absence means that goodbyes have been said or need to be said. Sometimes we missed out on expressing our goodbyes or we need to say it again. Even after our spouse is gone it is possible to complete the goodbye. The value is taking the time to express it.

Goodbyes are a major part of life. Some farewells are forced on us, while others are quite intentional. Some bring aches and deep sadness, and we strive to minimize or kill the pain. Goodbyes come in various intensities. Some are said with meaning, and others come out quite glibly. The word "goodbye" originally was "God be with ye" or "Go with God." It was a recognition that God was part of the journey. The expression was a blessing of love. That if God went with you, you would never be alone. His comfort and strength would be with you. And it's true! If we remember that he is with us always, we'll know we never travel alone.

Farewells and saying goodbye can be painful and harsh, but they can also include the comfort of God's presence.

Goodbyes leave an empty place in our hearts. There's an incompleteness, a space that says, "I want to be filled!" Have you ever had a hollow feeling in the pit of your stomach when you turn away from someone you've said goodbye to? Every loss we experience encompasses a goodbye. And when we've said goodbye to a spouse, the goodbyes tend to multiply and apply to many situations.[1]

Joyce Rupp, the author of *Praying Our Goodbyes,* said,

> We all need to learn how to say goodbye, to acknowledge the
> pain that is there for us so that we can eventually move on to

another hello. When we learn how to say goodbye we truly learn how to say to ourselves and to others, "Go, God be with you. I entrust you to God. The God of strength, courage, comfort, hope, love, is with you. The God who promises to wipe away all tears will hold you close and will fill your emptiness. Let go and be free to move on. Do not keep yourself from another step in your homeward journey."[2]

Your Reflections

1. How did you say goodbye to your spouse?

2. What do you wish you could have said?

3. What do you wish your spouse had said to you?

53

SAYING GOODBYE

If you need to say goodbye, what can you do? Many have found it helpful to write a goodbye or farewell letter. This may be an emotional experience for you, but it can bring you a sense of completeness. And that's the purpose of your letter—to *complete* your relationship. You may believe that it already was complete, and yet as you reflect upon it you may realize there were things you wish you'd said or done or wish your spouse had said or done. You're not alone in feeling like this.

It's good to be aware of how your relationship was incomplete. Accept the responsibility for your role in it being incomplete, and then contemplate what wasn't said that needs to be said.[1]

Think about the last conversation you had with your spouse. Can you remember it? I can remember my last talk with Joyce. I can also see it in my mind. A tumor in her brain burst and seemed to stop all meaningful conversation between the two of us. From then on our "conversation" was only one way—me talking and, hopefully, Joyce hearing and understanding.

As you think about your last conversation, where was it? Describe as best you can who said what. If possible put it in a dialogue format. Note whether it was an easy conversation or a difficult one and why.

Your purpose in writing this letter is to verbally wrap up those things you wish were different, better, or more in your relationship. How do you construct this letter? You can write this as if your spouse can hear you read it. Be thorough and don't be concerned about grammar or style.

What should you cover? Ask God to give you the memories you need to write this letter. Ask him for guidance on what to write. What was emotionally incomplete in your relationship? You can write about that. This letter writing may be difficult, but persevere. Remember, you're not writing about your spouse and what he or she might have done or didn't do. You're writing about *your* contribution in the incompleteness. Make the letter as long as it needs to be. Think of this as your last conversation with your spouse, so take your time...several days will allow time for more memories to surface. And you may find it helpful to use pictures to remind you of events and moments.

So many of us fail to say what we want or need to say when we're married. We end up living with regrets and "if onlys." This process can bring healing and hope to your life. It's a way of saying goodbye to the regrets, the emotional incompleteness, the lack of forgiveness, and the lack of "thank yous."

Would you like some specific help to get started? Here are some more ideas.

- What do you wish you had said emotionally?
- What do you wish you hadn't said emotionally?
- What do you wish you had thanked your spouse for?
- What do you wish you had forgiven him or her for?
- What do you wish your mate could have forgiven you for?

When you feel there is nothing more to say, you've finished. Close it by writing "I love you."

When you're done, choose a place to read your letter to your spouse. Where did he or she like to discuss important things with you? You can go to a favorite room or in a garden...anywhere that had meaning for the two of you. Some people go to the cemetery or where the ashes are kept.

When you read the letter imagine that your spouse is present in front of you. You can also place a picture of your spouse on a chair and sit in front of it if this helps you. Read with all the feeling you can. If the tears come, that's fine. Let it happen. Make sure you've allotted plenty of time since this may be a very emotional experience.

Don't listen to any negative thoughts that tell you "This is redundant" or "This is a waste of time." This process can be a very beneficial experience for you! It is well worth doing.

If you have a close supportive friend you may find it helpful to read it to him or her. Some people have found it beneficial to read their letters in a close-knit support group.

When you've concluded your reading, tell your spouse goodbye once again. You may want to say it in different ways or even wave.[2]

My Journal

Worship. Sunday morning. Quiet, the sun just breaking over the back fence and pushing through the haze. A time of worship in front of the TV, as it had been for the past 20 years. Today had a wondrous and uplifting hymn sung by a 300-voice choir accompanied by a 5-keyboard organ. A cat sat by one foot (hoping to be fed) and my dog at the other (hoping to be petted). This was an early Sunday morning routine that fed our souls. Joyce and I would sit and worship quietly without having to stand, listen to the twanging of a loud guitar, or sing so many words we didn't have a chance to let them speak to us.

I thought of those who spoke to us over the years—who encouraged us, enlightened us, and pointed us to the God who gives us strength and comfort. Lloyd Ogilvie, Adrian Rogers, Charles Stanley, and James Kennedy came to mind. And in the last three years David Jeremiah inspired us. Joyce would sit and listen, open her Bible, make comments, share what she learned…but not today. At least not here. She's learning and worshiping elsewhere. My mind tells me it's best. People tell me it is through what they say as well as in the cards they sent. But my heart says something else. I would like to see her in her chair with a cup of coffee by her side and her Bible open on her lap. Even that last Sunday before she lapsed into a coma she was here, struggling to grasp the teaching and write a few words. Her notes on sermons and teachings are scattered about in books, on pads, and in her Bible.

And so I sit with only the animals for companions, glancing now and then at her silent chair. I heard a new anthem this morning and wished she could have heard it and experienced the blessing of the words. But then the thought struck me, *Perhaps she is saying at this same moment, "Norm, I heard a new anthem this morning. I wish you could have heard it. Someday in the future, you will. We will together."*

54

TRANSITIONS

It's time. It's been a month since I've written anything. It's not that I haven't needed to write. Perhaps more than ever I need to, but emotionally I wasn't into remembering. But as I walked Shadow this evening, my mind drifted back to the beginning of this time in my life. It feels like the beginning of the end of a difficult journey. In my mind I see the trips and appointments to Cedar-Sinai Hospital and the visits to Joyce's oncologist and surgeons.

I've realized many things about myself as well as some uncertainties about me through this progression of grief. I wonder if there are times when I think or analyze or feel too much. I know I ask too many questions that can't be answered. My grief is moving and changing. I'm in transition, which was bound to happen. Is what I'm feeling okay? Should it be at this level now? I'm not sure. Everything seems different and less certain. The music I once listened to has a different effect upon me now. I know I've turned a corner, but that in itself brings a new set of losses. The memories aren't as sharp and neither are the images, which, in a way is all I have left after such a loss. After almost 50 years together shouldn't my feelings remain intense and vivid longer than this?

I'm discovering that I must have been carrying a low-grade grief fever during Joyce's illness. It was painful but not recognized as such. Did I know or believe it would end like this? Not consciously, at least. I probably wouldn't allow myself to believe it. Perhaps if I don't believe or think something I can keep it from happening. But magical thinking doesn't work as much as I'd like it to. So part of me knew what was coming and part of me wouldn't accept it.

I'm learning that healing comes when I reach out to help others. I've learned that I'm lonely...and I don't like being that way. I want companionship. I long for someone to converse with other than immediate family. But is that right? Is that okay? Where is the timetable of grief? Is there one? I debate what to do and say and which direction to go. It feels as though a part of me is stuck in the past, part is here in the present, and some of me is in the future.

Confusion reigns. Some say this is growth. I share some of what I'm thinking and feeling, but I'm not sure that everyone will understand and track with me. Yes, I know a lot about grief through my work, and that helped me during the first few months. But now I feel a bit more adrift and in the midst of uncharted waters wondering... sometimes just wondering...and waiting.

I'm finding a new sense of being out-of-control with my grief. I think I must have subconsciously had time lines constructed for where I would be in my grief at specific points. But grief refuses to be controlled. I'm still surprised by what happens and when it occurs, as well as when grief seems to have disappeared.

My Journal

Tonight I watched Joyce's memorial service recording for the first time. I procrastinated, hesitated, delayed, and finally pressed the play button. The tears came. But it was a different type of sadness...and difficult to explain. The emptiness came back.

I've always had difficulty and feel discomfort watching myself, and this was no exception as I saw myself at the service. But I watched anyway and heard who Joyce was once again.

Am I trying to reconnect to the feelings of the past to dampen what is occurring now and might in the future? I'm not sure—in fact, there's quite a lot I'm not sure of now.

Today I went to the gravesite because Joyce's marker had been placed. I went wondering what I would experience, but I felt emotionally flat. I was disappointed. I've been here before to place flowers, and some times had been very intense. Is this all there is now when it comes to remembering? Perhaps I'm trying to orchestrate what will trigger my sense of loss and when it happens, but I should know better. Grief doesn't work that way. Perhaps I'm worried that I'll forget Joyce and the deep love we shared.

The unexpected surprise of grief (June 1, 2008). They come one after another. The reminders of grief. They have a message to share. One that I'm aware of but that I'm trying to forget or hide or ignore. "You're alone. You're without your spouse, and she won't be back." There's a fresh bite of pain, and the grief becomes fresh and strong once again.

This time it came after I dropped a graduation card on the floor in the market. As I bent to retrieve it I glanced at the next section of cards. They were Father's Day cards. But the one I saw said "From Your Loving Wife," and I knew I wouldn't be receiving this card from Joyce now or ever again.

I got home and opened the mail and found an invitation from one of my publishers to a dinner at a convention. The invite was cleverly written and the location would be special. But if I went I wouldn't be with Joyce. Again "without."

If these only occurred one at a time, I could handle them better. But then again, perhaps not.

Last evening I sat at the grand piano playing some of the music Joyce enjoyed hearing. I also played one of the pieces I played for the background music for her DVD tribute. As I did a thought that had been fermenting in my mind for several days became clear. It's been about four months since the intense grief of the first four months lifted. When it did I was thrown off balance because I wasn't expecting it to fade so rapidly. I realized as I sat there playing that I was actually grieving the loss of my intense grief for Joyce. It was the grief that helped keep her real, which kept me connected. And now the connection was like a loose wire flapping in the breeze. My efforts to reconnect the wire were to no avail. I guess since I can't accomplish this, I have to let grief do it her own way and in her own time.

A good friend I shared this with said grief is like a hug from the person you've lost. And that's so true. As I sat and played and reflected, I could feel Joyce coming up behind me and putting her arms around me.

Concluding Thoughts

There are two words that were said thousands of times during my almost 50-year marriage to Joyce that I can and will continue to say to her: Thank you!

Thank you for...

- who you were as a person
- influencing and enriching my life in such positive ways
- being such a model of graciousness
- your love and faithfulness to the Word of God
- what you gave to Matthew, Sheryl, and Shaelyn
- loving me with a sacrificial love
- fulfilling my life in a way I never dreamed possible
- impacting thousands of people by who you were as much as by what you said...and this continues today
- giving me memories that will last forever

My "thank yous" will continue. And one day the difficult word "goodbye" will no longer be expressed by me. They will be replaced by "Hello, Joyce."

PERSONAL STORIES OF GRIEF RECOVERY

❧

GRIEF RECOVERY EVALUATION

❧

NOTES

I Don't Understand

I spent my twenty-fifth wedding anniversary in the beautiful purple majesty of the Rocky Mountains in Colorado with eight other people—none of them my husband. I lost Phil after 22 years of marriage. He was my high school sweetheart and my best friend. We vowed to "love, honor, and cherish each other as long as we both shall live." Neither of us ever considered the possibility that one of us would die young. Now I find myself a widow with a son to raise alone. And to put it bluntly, it stinks!

My husband developed cancer as a result of his job as a firefighter. By the time we discovered he'd been diagnosed and treated for the wrong cancer, it was too late. Though a new doctor believed he could help Phil, his weakened body gave up and his heart stopped. Nothing they tried to do revived him. We buried him on his forty-fifth birthday, six days before Christmas. It was a beautiful home-going complete with full firefighter honors. Phil was a faithful believer in Jesus Christ, and his funeral service shared the gospel message. But after all the hugs and well-wishes, I had to go home without my husband. Even though I'd slept alone many nights because of Phil's schedule, he always came home in the morning. That would never happen again.

I know the Lord prepared me for this loss in many ways. I look back and see the people who were there to guide the many decisions I had to make in those first few weeks. Our lawyer and accountant were friends of ours. The fire department walked us through a maze of paperwork. I was "adopted" by a Bible-study group at my church so all those "honey-dos" still got done. To this day I have many numbers

I can call for help. But I still have to do many jobs that "belonged" to my husband. Sometimes I resent having to do them. After all, wasn't marriage designed by God partly so two people could share the load? And yes, I may not enjoy it as much, but I know God will provide the strength or brawn I need.

I'm not the same person I was before my husband died. Just ask my son. He will tell you that I'm not as patient or as fun, and that I don't smile as much as I used to. I don't look at the world the same. My dreams have been shattered, and sometimes I find it hard to believe that God cares about me. He gave me the man of my dreams and then took him away much too soon. Phil and I never got to say good-bye. The doctor said he could treat the cancer. No one ever mentioned death. At the same time I *know* God cares about me because he shows it every day. He's provided for me financially and through friends and family. I am his child and he says he loves his children. I don't understand his plan for my life, and at the moment I don't particularly like it. Nevertheless, I trust God even when circumstances and emotions lead me to doubt. I know Phil is in heaven, and I know I will see him again one day. I know he is no longer suffering, and that makes me glad because his decline was so painful to watch. I still don't look forward to the future without him, and it hurts to know my son has to grow up without his father's godly influence. I wonder why God chose to take a good man out of this world when we need godly men more than ever. God's ways and purposes are definitely his own.

I'm learning to trust that God will continue to guide me, teach me, comfort me, and strengthen me each and every day as I face this journey chosen for me. Without God I wouldn't have healed as much as I have. Without God I couldn't make it through each challenging day. Without his promise of eternal life for those who believe in his Son Jesus, I would never have the hope of seeing Phil again. I look forward to seeing him as well as other family and friends when we stand together in the presence of our Lord and Savior Jesus Christ. Knowing that will happen gets me through each day and makes the future seem a little bit brighter.

Surprised by Grief

The title of C.S. Lewis' classic book *Surprised by Joy* has been rattling through my brain as I reflect on the loss of my husband, Bob, four years ago. For me *Surprised by Grief* seems to fit my experience to a "T."

Bob was admitted to the hospital for the last time (after countless admissions), a day after our thirty-fourth wedding anniversary. After a week in ICU he came home under hospice care for five days before he died. Our three daughters were all able to come home for the last week of his life. What a huge present God gave us, allowing us to go down memory lane and say goodbye and see Bob smile, which we hadn't seen for years. The inner peace that had eluded Bob his whole life was finally obvious in his eyes before he died. What a gift!

Bob's health had declined slowly and steadily over the previous five years due to lung problems, heart disease, and osteoporosis, aggravated by smoking and other destructive habits he couldn't seem to quit even after many attempts. As a physician he'd helped countless patients and was a role model to the residents he taught, yet he seemed powerless to help himself. In spite of all his talents, intelligence, and respect from patients, residents, and colleagues, his inner unhappiness led to increased anger toward himself, his world, and even us, his family. Bob was on oxygen 100 percent of the time the last year of life. As he could do less and less, he felt he had let God down and that his life had been a waste. That's what made the miracle of answered prayer so huge.

When Bob went "home," I knew he was at last 100 percent okay.

His body wasn't broken anymore. He knew at last how much he was loved and appreciated. And because so much of our life together was me trying to make him happy, and since Bob was finally okay, I was okay at last too. Not everyone gets to say goodbye, and seeing Bob smile and witnessing the peace in his eyes was a miraculous gift from God I didn't expect. How grateful I was. I thought finally all was well, and I would mostly be relieved and wouldn't need to grieve.

My emotional well-being has long been anchored in my faith and the music ministry God has given me for most of my adult life. As a church choir director, the privilege of active involvement in worship, music, and the choir family has been a blessing and a major tool that God used to strengthen and comfort me through the years. After Bob died, my involvement increased. I could now serve God 24/7 because my girls were all grown-up, and I no longer had a spouse to care for.

The surprise was how much I missed Bob and how much I was still a "we" in my heart. In so many ways we weren't a couple because we lived very separate lives: his medicine, my music; the stress of his anger toward me, especially when we became an empty nest. Our marriage had many trials over the years, and my promise before God to love "in sickness and health, joy and sorrow, better and worse" was what kept me going (plus the hope that God could work a miracle in our relationship).

By focusing on Bob all those years and trying not to let his anger hurt me, my heart had developed a protective wall I was completely unaware of. However, my body knew. My denial and working 24/7 caused chest pains. When I went to the doctor to find the source, to my surprise he said it was stress and not my heart.

When my best friend died of cancer 16 months after Bob, I went with her husband to a GriefShare class (so he would go because I thought I was okay). I was shocked to discover that I couldn't identify with any of the emotional reactions described. I learned that I was stuck in an emotional wasteland, that grief was a journey of the heart everyone must travel, and I hadn't even started, although Bob had died almost two years earlier. To think that all that time I thought I was okay simply because Bob was okay, but I was really running in circles and going nowhere! No wonder I still kept talking about Bob in every conversation.

Through the GriefShare videos, personal sharing, Bible study, and prayer, my heart finally began to crack. My feelings that I for too long thought were irrelevant returned. The pent-up dam of tears (that had caused my chest pains) opened up and flowed—and it felt good. Now I had a problem. I lost the stamina and mental energy to continue wearing my many hats (responsibilities). I needed a time-out to grieve and let my feelings carry me for a while.

That awareness led me to take a six-month sabbatical from all the hats I was wearing—church, school, community choir—everything! Everyone supported me and understood. In fact, several folks wondered why it took so long for my grief to catch up with me. The sabbatical was like one long vacation to visit family, friends, read, play, travel, rest, and recover my quiet time that had been squeezed out of my life for too long. I finally began to learn who I was.

The last two years have been a slow process of self-discovery (even exploring what I like to eat and where I want to go), which at first sounded so simple and selfish. But I've learned there is a huge difference between self-care and selfishness. Becoming self-aware has been quite revealing. I've learned so much I didn't know. My "new normal" is not what I expected, yet it is becoming wonderful. I'm gradually becoming comfortable with being by myself. Grief is a great teacher, especially in God's hands, and he does bring healing.

My pastor recognized my learning to live with joy again and asked me to lead GriefShare in my church. We're beginning our third series this fall. Every time is unique because the people who are grieving are unique. What is amazing is that as I try to help others find and receive God's comfort for living, he teaches me something new about myself.

My journey through the grief tunnel was delayed. Yet once I began I knew eventually I would reach daylight at the other end—healing and joy! Indeed, *Surprised by Grief* has been a blessing in my life, and I'm grateful for it.

REBUILDING THE EGG

The Bible says, "For this reason a man will leave his father and mother and be united with his wife, and they will become one flesh" (Genesis 2:24). "Well, God," I asked, "what am I supposed to do when she isn't here anymore?" We were together 34 years. Six weeks after diagnosis, Irene was gone.

At the beginning of grief I felt like I'd fallen into a deep well of water and was entangled in something that felt like heavy chains. Down and down and down I went. In one sense I thought I should be fighting to get back up to the surface where I could breathe. In another sense, I was thinking, *What's the use? Nothing's up there for me any longer.*

I was realizing that Irene's loss was so very much more than just the death of my loved one. It included the loss of our pet names and phrases for each other, her sound, the sight of her, her smell, her touch, her smile, her laugh. So many things were gone: our dreams and plans, the shared humor and comfort level we had with each other, the growth in achievements and failures, how we were complements to each other (many times as opposites); the ways we gave our support and encouragement; and just being each other's head cheerleader.

I was fortunate because in the previous couple of years we had worked to be current with "resolving not solving" several of our key issues and crises as a couple. So there wasn't a lot of guilt and regret I had to deal with when Irene got sick.

While my life settled into the ordinary, day-in and day-out look on the outside, percolating on the inside were so many feelings. And I don't recall any of them being the positive kind. I saw my life as an egg that had been thrown to the ground, like Humpty Dumpty pushed off the great wall. The egg broke into thousands of pieces scattered hither and yon, an accurate representation of my broken life. Each bit and piece represented the dreams, plans, desires, disappointments, downfalls, successes, tension, joy, and just plain life that happens in a committed marital relationship. It was nothing I could ever put back together again.

I decided to make the "shattered and scattered" egg my marker, the measuring stick used for watching for healing and growth. I would watch to see who, how, and what would put "this" egg back together. Over the many years of my healing I kept track of my progress by drawing that egg growing in size and in the shape I felt it was taking as I was getting put back together, tiny piece by tiny piece, sometimes one at a time and sometimes several pieces being placed back into the egg shape at once. It represents months and years of work being done in me.

A verse in Proverbs 23 stood out to me: "For as he thinks in his heart, so is he" (verse 7 NKJV). Well, I decided I wanted to get as much crummy stuff up and out from my insides as possible so God could deal with it. There was way too much anxiety, and I couldn't handle it on my own. Too much worry and insecurity for me to carry around by myself.

With this in mind, I tried to be as open and honest with the Lord as I could as I sought his comfort. I would *scream* out to him with the pains of frustration, anxiety, and emptiness. I did this daily, along with reading the Bible and various devotions, journaling, and sketching (sometimes just a simple face depicting what was going on in me at that time, such as feeling sad, mad, scared, confused). These times inspired my phone answering machine messages. I created well over 250 of them. I started putting messages on my answering machine because I was trying to be real and current and to let others know how much I was hurting and to ask for prayer. Also, many a time God would comfort me in my pain and give me reassurance through the Scriptures, especially in the book of Psalms.

God also used a community of people—a few couples, a few brave men—people he put into my life, many here to this day, who became wells for nourishment and nurturing. And he also placed me in a ministry to younger people. Another source of support was a friend from work. I was able to do much of my work from the house that first year, and this friend would call me periodically throughout the week to let me know when he was available and to see if I could use help doing anything at the office.

Another key component for healing was to meet regularly with a couple of men I trusted and with whom I could be very open and candid. With them I was accepted no matter where I was emotionally or spiritually. They were here for me.

Along the way I shed tears (it seemed like buckets of them) even though I knew Irene was with Jesus. God says he keeps track and counts all our tears (Psalm 56:8).

I designed thank-you notes to send to people. I drew the picture, wrote the salutation and message, and printed them. I wanted to personally thank people for their kindness, gifts, and thoughtfulness. It took a while, but this was very helpful in my healing process.

Grief counseling was important too. God really touched me at times in those sessions. When I finished my counseling, I decided to help start grief classes at our church, which we hadn't had before. I attended and helped facilitate these classes for more than two years. Also I read several books about grief and about cooking (more about that later).

A big deal for me was figuring out who I was…who "Dave" was. Since Irene and I were married when we were young and basically grew up together, I didn't really know who I was apart from her. I decided to visit some of the places and do some of the activities we'd done together. My intention was to see if I would do these on my own, as "a Dave thing," or to see if the activities and events were "Irene things," where I'd played a supportive role. Could these become a "Dave and someone else thing" sometime in the future? These times and activities were extremely difficult but very helpful when figuring out where "we" stopped and "I" started.

There were a couple of other activities I did that helped bring feelings to the surface and see what else I would be missing. These exercises gave my memories a historical context. First, I made a list of all that Irene was as I knew her. I listed everything about her I'd be missing. This helped to put her face and personality on my grief. Second, I did a time line with the positive and negative events of our life together, including the dates I could remember. This gave the years of our lives together meaning and perspective.

Reading cookbooks and taking cooking classes came about because Irene was a wonderful cook and I was missing that. The restaurant meals weren't cutting it, and I was hankering for some real comfort food. I came across her box of recipes so I got started. I'm nowhere near the cook she was, but I found myself enjoying it. I've been able to share my newfound joy with others. Plus, trading and sharing recipes is a way I can be involved with the opposite sex without interaction becoming an emotionally threatening situation. I've had a lot of fun cooking and exchanging recipes.

Once I started working out of the office again, I found it difficult to go back to the house, especially after a rough day. Sometimes I would pull into the driveway and be bushwhacked by overwhelming emotion. This caught me off guard and lasted for more than a couple of years. Finally it faded.

I called home "the house" for most of eight years because it didn't seem like home without Irene. Then one day while talking to one of my daughters, I said, "I'm heading *home*." Later I realized what I'd said and that it was the result of changes that had been taking place in me. This was a huge deal and had significant meaning for me. It meant I was accepting and becoming more comfortable and familiar in *my* space and place. It was OK for me to be and do there, whole and on my own.

The second and third years after Irene's death were much harder than the first. They were more intense because I was out of the shock and most of the denial. The differences between life with and without Irene were more apparent. I noticed the gaps in family gatherings.

Without her there to discuss plans and bounce ideas off of, I was afraid of making gaffs or mistakes I would have to live with. Like someone pelting me with tennis balls, these hits in the raw areas of my life stung and left a mark but caused little permanent damage. The one-on-one counseling was extremely helpful in moving me through these times. It helped having someone to talk to who understood where I was coming from and who was there to lend support and encouragement. My counselor helped me see what was headed my way and put together a plan so there might be fewer negative surprises down the road. He told me that for every five years of marriage, I could expect one year of grieving. It was seven to eight years of fading grief before I noticed the cloud of fog lifting and saw a future in my life.

After the third year in a devotional, I read, "You turned my wailing into dancing; you removed my sackcloth and clothed me with joy, that my heart may sing to you and not be silent" (Psalm 30:11-12). It took the better part of nine years to get most of the stuff and crud out. One day I realized I had arrived. I was whole, even if not all those little pieces of shell were in place, and even if there were cracks all over the egg. As I looked at that egg, I realized I'd been in a process where God was filling the space inside along with putting the shell back into place. There was room inside as I released all the grief and junk I was carrying around from all my losses and trying to handle it myself. God had been filling me with what he wanted for me. I've discovered life is a much lighter load. Now. Without Jesus Christ putting me back together, I *maybe* could have assembled the egg to some extent, but it would have been a fragile, egg-shaped shell without any internal substance. The Lord's focus on me was intentional and intense. He let me know that he could rebuild me alone, but he wanted us to do it together. Along the way and at various seasons and times, he's put people and ministries in my life to help me know that he is on my side and I am special to him.

Grief Recovery Evaluation

Place a mark on the line graphs to indicate where you are in your life right now. Date the marks so you can note your progress.[1] Complete this evaluation every three months or so.

Changes in Me Because of My Loss

1. I have returned to my normal levels of functioning in most areas of my life.

   0————————————5————————————10

2. My overall symptoms of grief have declined.

   0————————————5————————————10

3. My feelings do not overwhelm me when I think about my loss or when someone mentions it.

   0————————————5————————————10

4. Most of the time I feel all right about myself.

   0————————————5————————————10

5. I enjoy myself and what I experience without feeling guilty.

   0————————————5————————————10

6. My anger has diminished. When it occurs, I handle it appropriately.

0————————————5————————————10

7. I don't avoid thinking about things that could be or are painful.

0————————————5————————————10

8. My hurt has diminished, and I understand it.

0————————————5————————————10

9. I can think of positive things.

0————————————5————————————10

10. I have completed what I need to do about my loss.

0————————————5————————————10

11. Pain does not dominate my thoughts or life.

0————————————5————————————10

12. I can handle special days or dates without being overwhelmed by memories.

0————————————5————————————10

13. I have handled the secondary losses that accompanied my major loss.

0————————————5————————————10

14. I can remember the loss of my spouse on occasion without pain and without crying.

    0————————————— 5—————————————10

15. There is meaning and significance to my life.

    0————————————— 5—————————————10

16. I am able to ask the question "How?" rather than "Why?" at this time.

    0————————————— 5—————————————10

17. I see hope and purpose in life despite my loss.

    0————————————— 5—————————————10

18. I have energy and can feel relaxed during the day.

    0————————————— 5—————————————10

19. I no longer fight the fact that the loss has occurred. I have accepted it.

    0————————————— 5—————————————10

20. I am learning to be comfortable with my new identity and being without what I lost.

    0————————————— 5—————————————10

21. I understand that my feelings over the loss will return periodically. I understand and accept that.

    0————————————— 5—————————————10

22. I understand what grief means and have a greater appreciation for it.

0————————————5————————————10

Changes in My Relationship with My Spouse

23. I remember our relationship realistically with positive and negative memories.

0————————————5————————————10

24. The relationship I have with my lost partner is healthy and appropriate.

0————————————5————————————10

25. I feel all right about not thinking about the loss for a time. I am not betraying the one I lost.

0————————————5————————————10

26. I have a new relationship with my spouse. I know appropriate ways of keeping him or her "alive."

0————————————5————————————10

27. I no longer search for my loved one.

0————————————5————————————10

28. I don't feel compelled to hang on to the pain.

0————————————5————————————10

29. I can think about things other than my loved one.

0————————————5————————————10

30. My life has meaning even though my spouse is gone.

0————————————5————————————10

Changes I Have Made in Adjusting to My New World

31. I have integrated my loss into my world. I can relate to others in a healthy way.

0————————————5————————————10

32. I can accept the help and support of other people.

0————————————5————————————10

33. I am open about my feelings in my other relationships.

0————————————5————————————10

34. I feel it is all right for life to go on even though my spouse is gone.

0————————————5————————————10

35. I have developed an interest in people and things outside myself that have no relationship to the one I lost.

0————————————5————————————10

36. I have put my loss in healthy perspective.

0————————————5————————————10

Your Reflections

1. What did this evaluation tell you about your journey of grief?

NOTES

Chapter 1—The Disruption of Our Life Together

1. Adapted from Pamela Blair and Brook Noel, *I Wasn't Ready to Say Goodbye* (Naperville, IL: Sourcebook, Inc., 2008), p. 32.
2. Martha Hickman, *Healing After Loss* (New York: Collins Living, 1994).

Chapter 3—Time and Your Future

1. Adapted from Pamela Blair and Brook Noel, *I Wasn't Ready to Say Goodbye* (Naperville, IL: Sourcebook, Inc., 2008), p. 9.

Chapter 4—Am I Normal?

1. Adapted from Joann Jozefowski, *The Phoenix Phenomenon* (Northvale, NJ: Jason Aronson, 1999), p. 17.

Chapter 6—Caution—Fragile

1. Adapted from Pamela Blair and Brook Noel, *I Wasn't Ready to Say Goodbye* (Naperville, IL: Sourcebook, Inc., 2008), p. 13.

Chapter 12—Alive in Your Memory

1. Adapted from Pamela Blair and Brook Noel, *I Wasn't Ready to Say Goodbye* (Naperville, IL: Sourcebook, Inc., 2008), p. 170.

Chapter 13—A New Relationship

1. Adapted from Therese A. Rando, Ph.D., *Grieving: How to Go on Living When Someone You Love Dies* (Lexington, MA: Lexington Books, 1988), pp. 231-34.

Chapter 14—Never Enough

1. Adapted from John James and Frank Cherry, *The Grief Recovery Handbook* (New York: Harper & Row, 1988), pp. 109-21.

Chapter 15—What You Remember

1. Adapted from Therese A. Rando, Ph.D., *Grieving: How to Go on Living When Someone You Love Dies* (Lexington, MA: Lexington Books, 1988), p. 251.

Chapter 16—You're Still Alive

1. Adapted from Therese A. Rando, Ph.D., *Grieving: How to Go on Living When Someone You Love Dies* (Lexington, MA: Lexington Books, 1988), pp. 18-19.

Chapter 20—Reasons for Grief

1. Therese A. Rando, Ph.D., *Grieving: How to Go on Living When Someone You Love Dies* (Lexington, MA: Lexington Books, 1988), pp. 79-80.

Chapter 21—Feelings of Grief

1. Gay Hendricks, *Learning to Love Yourself,* quoted in Pamela Blair and Brook Noel, *I Wasn't Ready to Say Goodbye* (Naperville, IL: Sourcebook, Inc., 2008), pp. 75-76.

Chapter 25—Fears

1. Pamela Blair and Brook Noel, *I Wasn't Ready to Say Goodbye* (Naperville, IL: Sourcebook, Inc., 2008), p. 47.

Chapter 26—Depression and Grief

1. H. Norman Wright, *The New Guide to Crisis and Trauma Counseling* (Ventura, CA: Regal Books, 2003), p. 112.

Chapter 27—Avoiding Pain

1. Adapted from Pamela Blair and Brook Noel, *I Wasn't Ready to Say Goodbye* (Naperville, IL: Sourcebook, Inc., 2008), p. 63.
2. Ibid., pp. 76-77.

Chapter 28—I Believe

1. Raymond R. Mitsch and Lynn Brookside, *Grieving the Loss of Someone You Love* (Ventura, CA: Regal Books, 1993), pp. 58-60.
2. David W. Wiersbe, *Gone but Not Lost* (Grand Rapids, MI: Baker Books, 1992), p. 55.

Chapter 29—Relearning Your Life

1. Adapted from Susan J. Zonnebelt-Smeenge, R.N., Ed.D., and Robert C. De Vries, D.Min, Ph.D., *Getting to the Other Side of Grief* (Grand Rapids, MI: Baker Books, 1998), p. 181.
2. Adapted from Ann Kaiser Stearns, *Living Through Personal Crisis* (Chicago: Thomas More Press, 1984), pp. 85-86.
3. Adapted from Pamela Blair and Brook Noel, *I Wasn't Ready to Say Goodbye* (Naperville, IL: Sourcebook Inc., 2008), p. 80.

Chapter 30—Not Quite Myself

1. Original source unknown.

2. Adapted from Dale and Juanita Ryan, *Recovery from Loss* (Downer's Grove, IL: InterVarsity Press, 1990), pp. 40-41.

Chapter 32—A Look at Me

1. Adapted from Thomas Attig, *How We Grieve* (New York: Oxford University Press, 1996), pp. 111-21.
2. Adapted from Therese A. Rando, Ph.D., *Grieving: How to Go on Living When Someone You Love Dies* (Lexington, MA: Lexington Books, 1988), pp. 284-86.

Chapter 33—The Gift of Writing

1. Adapted from Susan J. Zonnebelt-Smeenge, R.N., Ed.D., and Robert C. De Vries, D.Min, Ph.D., *Getting to the Other Side of Grief* (Grand Rapids, MI: Baker Books, 2006), pp. 66-67.
2. Adapted from suggestions created and compiled by Dave Nair. Used by permission.
3. Dave Nair. Used by permission.

Chapter 36—Unresolved Grief

1. Charlotte A. Greeson, Mary Hollingsworth, and Michael Washburn, *Grief Adjustment Guide: A Pathway Through Pain* (Westminster, MD: Doubleday Religious Publishing Group, 2001).
2. Adapted from Terry L. Martin and Kenneth J. Doka, *Men Don't Cry...Women Do* (Philadelphia: Brunner/Mazell, 2000), pp. 35-52.
3. Adapted from Lilly Singer, Margaret Sirot, and Susan Rodd, *Beyond Loss* (New York: E.P. Dutton, 1988), pp. 82-83.

Chapter 37—The Last Time We Were Together

1. Adapted from R. Scott Sullender, *Losses in Later Life* (New York: Paulist Press, 1989), p. 115.

Chapter 43—Fighting Your Grief

1. This "Communicating with Your Grief" exercise is adapted from Bob Deits, *Life After Loss* (Tucson: Fisher Books, 1988), pp. 98-94, 146-47.

Chapter 44—Helping Others Help You

1. H. Norman Wright, *The New Guide to Crisis and Trauma Counseling* (Ventura, CA: Regal Books, 2003), pp. 116-17.
2. Source unknown.
3. Laurie J. Spector, M.S.W., and Ruth Spector Webster, M.S.W., *Lost My Partner—What'll I Do?* (Manhattan Beach, CA: McCormick Press, 1999), pp. 83-85.

Chapter 48—Caregiver—A Privilege

1. Adapted from Deborah S. Levinson, *Surviving the Death of Your Spouse* (Oakland, CA: New Harbinger Publishers, 2004), pp. 9-10.

Chapter 49—Anticipatory Grieving

1. Adapted from Martin M. Auz and Maureen Lyons Andrews, *Handbook for Those Who Grieve* (Chicago: Loyola Press, 2002), pp. 14-15.

Chapter 52—The Importance of Goodbye

1. Adapted from Joyce Rupp, *Praying Our Goodbyes* (New York: Ivy Books, 1988), pp. 7-23.
2. Ibid., pp. 20-21.

Chapter 53—Saying Goodbye

1. Adapted from John James and Frank Cherry, *The Grief Recovery Handbook* (New York: Harper and Row, 1988), pp. 152-53.
2. Adapted from ibid., pp. 154-59.

Grief Recovery Evaluation

1. Adapted from Therese A. Rando, *Grieving* (Lexington, MA: Lexington Books, 1988), pp. 231-34.

OTHER HARVEST HOUSE BOOKS BY
H. NORMAN WRIGHT

RELATIONSHIPS

101 Questions to Ask Before You Get Engaged

After You Say "I Do"

After You Say "I Do" Devotional

Before You Remarry

Before You Say "I Do"®

Before You Say "I Do"® Devotional

Finding the Right One for You

Quiet Times for Couples (hardcover)

Quiet Times for Those Who Need Comfort